MAKE
CONNECTIONS
COUNT!

THE SIX-STEP
SYSTEM TO
BUILD YOUR
MEGANETWORK™

MELISSA GIOVAGNOLI

Dearborn
Financial Publishing, Inc.

While a great deal of care has been taken to provide accurate and current information, the ideas, suggestions, general principles and conclusions presented in this text are subject to local, state and federal laws and regulations, court cases and any revisions of same. The reader is thus urged to consult legal counsel regarding any points of law—this publication should not be used as a substitute for competent legal advice.

The terms *MegaNetwork* and *MegaNetworking* are used throughout this work and are subject to application for federal trademark registrations, submitted as of August 25, 1994.

Publisher: Anita A. Constant
Executive Editor: Bobbye Middendorf
Managing Editor: Jack L. Kiburz
Associate Editor: Karen A. Christensen
Interior Design: Professional Resources & Communications, Inc.
Cover Design: Paul Perlow Design

Published by Dearborn Financial Publishing, Inc.

Printed in the United States of America

95 96 97 10 9 8 7 6 5 4 3 2 1

Library of Congress Cataloging-in-Publication Data

Giovagnoli, Melissa.
    Make your connections count!: the six-step system to build your MegaNetwork/Melissa Giovagnoli.
        p. cm.
    Includes bibliographical references and index.
    ISBN 0-7931-1151-X:
    1. Success in business. 2. Businessmen—Social networks. 3. Social networks. 4. Public relations. I. Title.
HF5386.G48 1995
650.1'3—dc20

94-26909
CIP

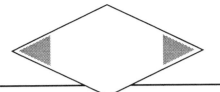

Dedication

To my family, my special MegaNetwork.

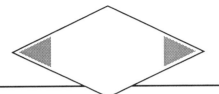

Acknowledgments

First I want to thank all the wonderful people at Friedman, Eisenstein, Raemer and Schwartz (FERS) and Practice Development Institute (PDI) who allowed me to use them as human guinea pigs to continuously improve the MegaNetworking system. Special thanks also to Lori Pedelty, a dynamic and incredibly accomplished consultant who was and still is my mentor and coach.

I especially appreciate all those who contributed insight and material: Janet Hansen, Sue Masaracchia, Lindsey Novak, Jim Pullano, Vicki Spina, Jeff Willinger and many more whose names are mentioned in the book. Additional praise must go to Sue Klokkenga whose editorial assistance was beyond excellent and Linda Catomer, my typist, who taught me that transcribing could be a sublime experience.

And then there's the wonderful team at Dearborn Financial Publishing, Inc. Bobbye Middendorf, my editor, was consistent, persistent and challenging, while simultaneously being kind and generous. She truly has a gift for working with writers.

Of course, with a family like I come from, where networking began at age five, I would be remiss if I didn't mention my wonderful networking sister, Cindy Goodman, whose weekly calls kept me focused. My other wonderful networking sister, Cari Goodman, kept me posted on articles that had anything to do with networking, and my brother, Greg Goodman, kept me busy with speaking engagements for the organizations where he is a member. My father Al Goodman, is the quintessential networker. Past president of his local Lion's Club and active in community organizations in the terrific town of Mansfield, Ohio, dad is constantly creating friendships. Then there is my mother, Marna Goodman, whose sincere interest in my work provided a special sounding board for my ideas.

Finally, I owe a special heartfelt acknowledgment to my two sons, Graham and Gavin and my wonderful husband, Steve. The three of them gave me my space for six months of writing nights and weekends. When people would ask me, "How do you do it all—take care of a family and still work and write?" I had to tell them the truth—I didn't. Steve and the boys really took care of me as well as themselves. They deserve credit, praise and most of all, my love.

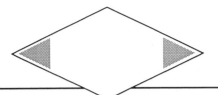

Contents

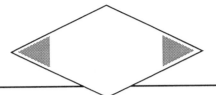

Introduction

For the past seven years, I have dedicated my efforts to learning everything I could about resources and relationships. I chose to become an entrepreneur—a nontraditional path to follow after finishing law school—because it was something I had always wanted to do. Creating a unique service—a referral service for tradespeople—I grew my business very quickly to the point where I had six full-time employees, two part-time employees, twelve-hundred square feet of office space and hundreds of headaches. I experienced what it was like to manage eight people, put in thousands of dollars of my own money and feel the excitement of the entrepreneur who wants to build a dynasty while also interacting with a husband, a home and two children. Three years after startup, I came to a fork in the road. Building to a point where I received national attention for the referral service, I was featured in one magazine that brought more than 100 letters from people around the country, including Alaska and Hawaii, who wanted to start businesses similar to mine. It was my chance to evolve. I chose to downsize my company, went back to working out of my home office and became a consultant on how to start referral services like mine.

Rather than franchise my concept, however, I began to sell what I called "packages" that ranged in price from $1,500 to $5,000 depending on the amount of consulting needed. I had experience consulting with large corporations, I had started and grown my own business and I had taught college. I had my share of managing people. I enjoyed consulting most of all.

I welcomed the opportunity to share what I had learned, helping others to avoid my mistakes and capitalize on the things I knew worked. I thought it was wonderful to help others step over the land mines that every small business faces. I knew I could improve their success. This desire turned into my life's mission. Four years later, I am still committed to helping entrepreneurs start and grow businesses. It is my belief that entrepreneurs embody creativity and hope for the future.

I started teaching self-employment training and began helping small businesses with everything from marketing and sales to strategic planning and financing. I read hundreds of books on all of these subjects. I became active in my city and state governments, as well as the Small Business Administration. I volunteered to work with my state's business development centers, offering free counseling to entrepreneurs. I donated hundreds of dollars to scholarships that sponsored self-employment training for underemployed and unemployed workers. Then I turned to writing books. As a former writing teacher who had been a business and technical writer, I had always wanted to write a book. I created my first book, *The Chicago Entrepreneur's Sourcebook* with the help of one of my self-employment training students. The book is a wonderful tool for learning about the huge number and quality of resources available to entrepreneurs, job seekers and sales professionals.

I became an expert on resources, both locally and nationally, and was asked to speak on the topics covered in *Sourcebook*. As my speaking engagement requests grew, I began to consider writing a second book. Good writers know that success in writing starts with knowing not only what peoples' needs are today, but what they will be when your book comes out a year later. I continued looking and listening, and I found that I was usually invited to speak about marketing topics. It was great to focus on planning and financing, but if entrepreneurs couldn't sell their products, they wouldn't have to worry about financing and planning.

Again, I learned a number of things about marketing and sales. Basic to what I learned is that our world is changing dramatically, and today's sophisticated consumers demand quality service.

At PDI, the accounting consulting firm where I now work, we know that customers can be very fickle. We found that a few years ago, clients of an accounting firm considered for acquisition would have been valued at $2 \frac{1}{2}$ times their annual revenues. Such firms are now worth half that amount. In other words, relationships carry much less weight today. This obviously has a dramatic effect on every company's bottom line.

My research taught me that marketing efforts have to be unconditionally dedicated to relationship building. I learned that success in relationship building requires a focus on interpersonal effectiveness. The umbrella term for this form of marketing is *networking*. Others have used phrases like *relationship marketing*, or *strategic or consultative selling*. I like the term networking because it is commonly used across the country. You can't pick up a business paper today that doesn't have the term networking somewhere. Less than three years ago local Chambers of Commerce would hesitate to use the term, but today most Chambers have more than one type of networking event (e.g., networking after-hours, networking president's forums, networking seminars, networking breakfasts or lunches).

I decided to test market my theory that networking was the best marketing strategy available for anyone responsible for marketing and selling a product, a service or themselves (job seekers and careerists). Within 6 months I booked 44 speaking engagements on the subject of networking. Everywhere I turned, someone was seeking advice on how to network to get a job or acquire a key account. Sales professionals, used to traditional cold calling techniques, wanted to know why there was so much excitement about networking.

In the midst of all this interest, I approached my publisher with the idea of writing a book on networking. Twelve months later, here it is. This book represents more than 500 hours of research and writing. For the past year, I have had the good fortune of working as a full-time networking coach and seminar leader. And because the firm that hired me is very entrepreneurial, I still have all the freedom of being my own boss.

I'm doing what I love the most. Through seminars, speaking engagements and one-on-one coaching sessions, I work with individuals and teams to build relationships that result in long-term sales success. I use the networking strategies that have worked for me and others to create a system that gives *twice* the results of current marketing and sales strategies in *half* the time. I call this the MegaNetworking™ System because it is quite different from traditional networking.

Some people think that networking has to be a serendipitous activity. If you see it only that way, you severely limit your chances to build a strategic network. Who should you pursue? Where? When? How? Networkers often *react* to the contacts they meet serendipitously. However, you can miss many quality contacts this way, ending up with Rolodexes® filled with contacts you seldom, if ever, reconnect with to build more effective relationships.

Effective networking is *not* a crowded Rolodex. It is a well thought out system for growing a business or a career. This book will help you learn how to avoid using a "hit or miss" methodology. Instead, you will create a simple action plan to *locate* and develop networks that are powerful and generate continuous referrals.

You will learn to build rapport with people very quickly by being introduced warmly by someone who knows someone who knows someone. You will also learn how to encourage your contacts to open up and brainstorm with you to make connections that generate good prospects. You will learn how to grow a relationship to exchange information, leads, referrals and emotional and promotional support. Working through the chapters, you will be able to more easily follow through on your promises, share your knowledge and resources, become an active listener, stay open to new ideas, keep asking questions that generate new prospects, compliment sincerely and learn to create a balanced exchange of referrals.

Life's lessons keep bringing us back to the need to make and nurture our connections. There is no benefit in taking more than we give—or giving without asking for a return. I am often reminded of my grandmother, one of the greatest people I have had the privilege of knowing. She sacrificed for everyone else's benefit. Now, many years after her death, I still remember the wonderful, kind things she did. I also remember that her dreams were never fulfilled. If my grandmother had allowed a more balanced exchange with others, she and those she helped would have benefited. My grandmother never learned how to encourage and educate others to share with her.

Exchanging with others should become your focus. It's the first step in establishing relationships. Keep in mind, however, that you won't realize an immediate benefit from all of your networking. The benefit might come later—from a person your initial contact directed you to or that person's recommended contact. It often takes a year or two or more for an exchange to develop.

In *Think and Grow Rich*, the classic book dealing with creating and building wealth, author Napoleon Hill talks about the secret to amassing an unlimited fortune. Andrew Carnegie—one of the richest men who ever lived—used this secret to become wealthy and powerful. As Hill puts it, the secret begins with the premise that all riches and achievements start with an idea. Your ideas are connected to your will, which in turn is connected to your actions.

If you consistently focus on achieving more than you are currently achieving, you will eventually realize your goals. Since Hill's groundbreaking work, hundreds of positive thinking books have brought their authors millions of dollars. From Norman Vincent Peale to W. Clement Stone to Zig Ziglar to Og Mandino, great teachers have shown us how our ideas form both our attitudes and our quality of life. The bottom line is: as we learn to control our thoughts, we will learn how to change them. When we replace unempowering thoughts with empowering ones, we choose a new path—a path that will lead us to the greatest gain.

Think about it. Imagine yourself in the home you always dreamed you'd have. Your workplace is just as wonderful. Now, see your relationships. Everyone you encounter has something pleasant to say. They notice your comfortable and attractive new clothes. They welcome your ideas and constantly thank you for them. Everyone is productive and happy. You share your thoughts and ideas, constantly creating new opportunities for yourself and others. You don't worry because you have so many new opportunities to do business, to grow your career, to build new relationships. You pick only the opportunities that are the most appealing to you at this point in your life. You're having fun. You're happy. You feel fulfilled.

This vision can be your new reality. We live in the *decade of the relationship*. Today, many specialists promote relationship building as the foundation for happiness. For all of the dreams that you hold, for all of the opportunities that you build, you will create strong relationships of trust.

Businesses don't strengthen our economy; people do. If you look deep into the structure of any company, you will find a few people at the top influencing the attitudes and the actions of all the others. How much influence those leaders have depends on the choices made by their employees. Many people today are free-thinkers. But there are many others who feel that they're trapped by their circumstances. Such people are in their own prisons, the prisons of their limited minds.

Renowned journalist Charles Kuralt, author of many books including *A Life on the Road* and former co-host of the award winning *Sunday Morning Program*, said during a recent speech that he has never seen a time in the last 20 years when Americans have been as supportive of one another. In the 1980s, the *decade of materialism*, it was a jungle out there. Today, it's truly different.

Yes, there is crime, increased violence and increased stress as the result of our poor economy. There are, however, many signs that a new wave of optimism is springing forth. Some consider this a time of renaissance. Opportunities are everywhere to capitalize on the development and management of information.

The key is to change your attitude by *adapting* rather than *resisting* change. But, be selective. Focus on those people who share your vision of what good relationships should be. Don't bother with anyone who *can't* or *won't* offer you similar support. Learn to recognize a no-win situation.

Our values are the source of our actions. Probe to learn the values of those with whom you build relationships. For me, integrity and follow-through are most important. What matters to you?

Most of all, stay aware. An acronym I use for AWARE is Attention With Action Realizes Excellence. Remember, you're building a lifetime network. There will always be opportunities to build relationships. Some will last for weeks, months or years. Others will exist for a lifetime.

Demand Quality Over Quantity

Many business owners and sales professionals I have met share a similar awareness—it is as difficult to acquire a $500 client as it is to acquire a $20,000 client. Think BIG! Sometimes it will take longer to get to the decision maker—but people at the top can be just as open as people below them. In fact, many MegaNetworkers I have talked to have found people at the top much easier to access.

Don't allow yourself to be intimidated by the prestige of another. Separate *who you are* from *what you do*. Realize that relationships grow over time and that it's really those shorter, periodic exchanges that keep a relationship building. The emphasis is on staying connected and staying consistent. Throughout this book, using the MegaNetworking System, I will show you how to take all the tips and strategies that are available for building relationships and put them into an easy, efficient, effective system. It is a system that will bring you unlimited potential whether you're in sales, seeking a new job, or looking at improving any of your relationships. You'll find a bigger win—a win where you benefit, the other party benefits and you actually co-create something that you could never have created individually.

This system will eliminate the problem of being over-committed, attending too many events, looking for the next great contact or prospect. You will have more time to enjoy the quality people in your network who share common values and interests.

The MegaNetworking System will show you how to make your connections count. Whether you are building relationships personally or professionally, you will maximize the time you spend by focusing on this process. You will find yourself and those with whom you interact more fulfilled and eager to build long-lasting relationships. By adding a natural structure and process to your daily interactions with others, you will create the quality of life in a world filled with increasing opportunities.

Make Your Connections Count focuses on the process of creating and developing new business and career opportunities through networking. Through MegaNetworking you will learn how to make your current contacts the foundation for a lifetime network of referrals. You will also learn how to build new relationships easily and effectively. The MegaNetworking System has been developed to help you create, manage and maintain beneficial, rewarding relationships with others. Whether you're an entrepreneur, a sales professional looking for a new base of customers, a job seeker or a *careerist* intent on growing or transitioning in your career, you will find MegaNetworking a great alternative to traditional networking processes.

Make Your Connections Count presents an optimum networking system, which is simple and incredibly effective—but *only* if you *use* it. Take the time to learn the process and understand its powerful benefits. Networking works *with* your natural abilities. You will use your own style to create a strong, viable network of support and new business opportunities. Your unique strengths and values will become the foundation of your success.

Networking
Trends and
Troubles

People typically use networks to generate new business opportunities, clients or customers and to build their careers. Career building includes transitioning from jobs, looking at new career development opportunities and choosing to move into a new career. Today, more than ever, the only constant is change. Continuous change can be seen clearly in business, where flexible work hours, employee leasing, outsourcing and consulting are commonly replacing traditional employee relationships. These dramatic changes in the workforce are creating dramatic changes in our relationships.

Building Relationships

It's important to build relationships that go beyond your current employment situation. In the near future, the word *project* may one day replace the word *job*. More and more companies will be hiring for short-term projects. As your work environment changes, you can adjust and even thrive if you make connections—build relationships. Connect with people who will be resources for you and you for them as you move from project to project rather than from job to job.

Learning To MegaNetwork

I define MegaNetworking as "the co-creation of new opportunities through an exchange of ideas, opportunities, actions or support." Co-creation is different from creating on one's own. When you *co-create*, you and a proactive referral source build new connections to influential sources through a consistent series of *exchanges*. Exchanges are semi-formal meetings, either in person or by phone, where the involved parties share resources. For example, you may have just read an article on a new product or company that would be of interest to your source; you share your information and your source reciprocates with the resources (information, leads, referrals, etc.) you are seeking. The focus is on encouraging an equal exchange where both parties realize a benefit to having shared.

Co-creation and sharing are just starting points. You must work with others to master the exchange. (Chapter 6 is dedicated to an in-depth description of this process.) Learning to master the exchange can dramatically improve your networking results as you educate others to proactively share the resources they gather on an ongoing basis. Both you and your sources will discover that it takes less effort to generate new business opportunities. You will identify contacts for your sources as they identify new resources for you. You can also take advantage of the existing relationships your sources have built to acquire further resources or introductions to people you would like to meet. You and your sources can also help each other find out whom you should be talking to, why you should be talking to them, when you should talk to them and what would be the best way to approach them.

The MegaNetworking process will help you dramatically accelerate your marketing, sales or job finding efforts. The more you MegaNetwork, the more you will identify new opportunities that result from less and less effort. How does this happen?

When you master the underlying process of effective networking, you create a system that rivals every marketing strategy in existence today. In order to accomplish this, you first need to learn the structure of networking and second, teach it to others.

Focus on People

Shift your focus to the people you do business with or the people you work with, rather than the companies they represent. Focusing on people rather than titles or companies creates the strong, effective relationships that are essential to creating and maintaining a MegaNetwork. Your success at developing new business opportunities and your personal satisfaction will increase as you learn to surround yourself with supportive, proactive people.

Unlike traditional networking, today's emphasis is on *quality* rather than *quantity*. So often we hear people talking about building that Rolodex or adding to that database—continually building a base of names and collecting business cards. These people have difficulty managing their time and contacts. They fail to return phone calls even from others who might be looking to do business with them. They are too busy trying to acquire even more new contacts! Soon this cycle becomes overwhelming.

I often see networkers who have hundreds of old business cards stuffed into their desks waiting to be used at some distant date. The boom in networking over the past five years has resulted in thousands of people in casual, short-term relationships who seem to have a constant need to meet even more people. This "hit-or-miss" approach has created more frustration than anything else.

When your emphasis is on the number of people you meet rather than the quality of your relationships, you are traveling down a path that leads to frustration. The Pareto Principle states that 20 percent of your efforts will yield 80 percent of your results. Start by identifying your current contacts, and use them as a base to introduce you to similar contacts. Most people don't make this association.

Meeting and Greeting

You're probably as inundated as I am with invitations to join new associations and participate in new networking. There are numerous opportunities to meet and greet people. This emphasis on meeting and greeting, though, takes us away from the development of a strong network. The development of a MegaNetwork that is focused on quality will generate the business opportunities you seek TWICE as fast in HALF the time.

How My Garden Grew

When I was first married, my husband and I lived in a condominium. We had the unique opportunity of turning what was initially a whole row of aquariums into terrariums. I'm not much of a fish lover, but I did have a father who was a florist and one of his specialties was terrariums. After looking at these big fish tanks, I called

Dad for help. We put in grow lights, gravel and soil, even mirrors to make the tanks look bigger. We ended up with six large terrariums that filled the length of one wall of our basement. Finally, we added a variety of domestic and wild flowers.

Every day I would go down to the basement to see how the plants were progressing. After a month or so, we were delighted to see a healthy, beautiful assortment of exotic and domestic plants and flowers. What happened next, however, was totally unexpected.

Our flowers continued to grow until they resembled a lush prehistoric garden. We had created the perfect growth environment. As the plants flourished, we witnessed one of the most beautiful sights I've ever seen—one huge terrarium after another filled with hundreds of plants and flowers spilling over with color and fragrance.

This is how you want your network to grow! Make sure that you have just the right number of people to network with on a regular basis, then stay in contact with each other. Building solid relationships over time will bring the best results—continuous referrals and lasting friendships.

The Hidden Network

To develop relationships, you must turn your *Hidden Network*—the contacts behind your contacts—into referral sources. Good referral sources will be proactive rather than reactive. Reactive sources wait for other people to ask them if they know of anyone who could fill a certain position, take on a certain job responsibility, business opportunity or business service, or sell a particular product. Proactive networkers, on the other hand, are constantly looking for new opportunities. These are the people who place you in a top position in their network.

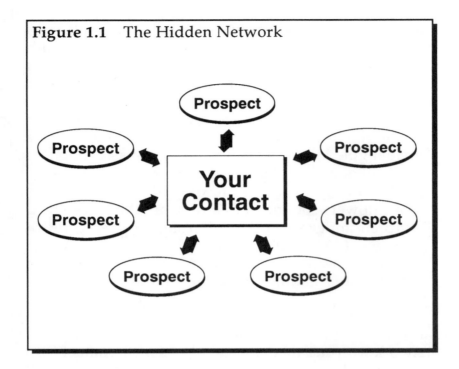

Figure 1.1 The Hidden Network

They care about you. They actively promote you to anyone and everyone that they meet.

Too often people focus on a contact as a prospect, rather than as a Hidden Network, a *conduit* to other prospects. Whenever you meet someone, ask yourself if that person is a proactive networker who has influence with others.

The ability to influence comes from being aware of the needs of others. Good influencers are attentive to other peoples' needs. They are constantly looking and inquiring on your behalf. They represent your interests. They are also people who take action. They have no problem saying, "Can I give you the name of someone?" or "Why don't I have my associate call you?"

Influencers are constantly developing new relationships and looking to see what potential there is for you to be working with them. Proactive people are givers, and in turn, they end up receiving as well.

Your Primary Network

When you're working with the 80-20 Rule, it's easy. You don't have to remember a lot of people. Start with your primary network, which is comprised of your referral sources. This network can consist of as few as two or three people. Most of the MegaNetworkers I interviewed had no more than ten key referral sources in their primary network. They only need a few referral sources who have power networks that reach wide and deep. Once you develop your primary network, you can build your secondary network of more casual sources and contacts.

Another problem with traditional networking is the lack of a big picture perspective. You need to know where to find referral sources and *influencers*—people with influence. These people *are* accessible; you can locate them through industry publications, associations, general business publications that run weekly success stories or just general publications that focus on affluent people. (Don't make the mistake of believing, however, that all affluent people are influential.)

Influential people have relationship power and can choose to use this power to introduce you to those with whom they have the strongest amount of influence. Not everyone the influentials introduce you to will be the type of people with whom you want to network. Building a diverse network will help you access a better primary network. And things change. Someone you network with today might not be someone you will network with a year or two from now. Conversely, someone you *don't* network with now might be someone you will network with regularly in the future.

From Fear to Accomplishment

Sometimes you'll need to work on overcoming natural barriers or phobias to effective networking. If you have these fears, you can overcome them by moving from the fear of rejection to the thrill of accomplishment. You can overcome your initial fear (many have stated that a certain amount of fear never goes away) as you learn that we can accomplish much more than we might have anticipated. Chapter 5 contains tips, strategies and methodologies for overcoming the fear of rejection. You will also learn how to turn apprehension into the anticipation of new opportunities. Throughout the book, you will learn how to look at the bigger picture—the type of networking pattern you are creating. You will learn how to avoid judging others' comments, behavior and appearance and instead, look for qualities to appreciate and acknowledge. You will learn the language of appreciation.

What's in It for You?

Another problem with traditional networking is the dissatisfaction people have with their current networking efforts. I remember one woman in a networking group that I was involved in, when asked how she enjoyed the group and whether she found it beneficial said, "I've gone the whole year, but I've given the most and gotten the least."

When I see someone in this situation, I realize that there are far too many people out there who take months looking for the perfect referral. The time involved in networking can be significantly decreased if you start slowly. Begin with one good referral source and through introduction after introduction, network to the most proactive contacts with the best referrals.

Don't make the mistake of networking only when you are desperate. The time to network is when you don't need it. A good example of a consistent networker is Vicki Spina, author of *Getting Hired in the '90s*.

Vicki tells the story of a human resource professional who saved her company more than $200,000 one year by continuously networking rather than conducting traditional job searches. By building an existing base of contacts for a wide variety of jobs at her company, this specialist learned the different capabilities, interests and current job status of her sources. She was then able to tap into her network whenever she needed a position filled.

Ineffective Networking

Ineffective networking can also cause social suicide. One banking officer said to me, "I'm very concerned about the commercial lenders in my bank. I realize that if they're not networking right, they could actually be harming our bank or the reputation of our bank that we've worked so hard to achieve."

Networking isn't just about getting out there, making contacts and meeting and greeting people. It goes much further. It involves nurturing solid, long-lasting relationships based on integrity, caring and a real interest in partnering.

Repeat and Refer

Larry Wilson, president and CEO of Pecos River Learning Center and author of the *Changing the Game: The New Way to Sell*, says that no business today can succeed without two things: repeat business and referred business. When you build your own MegaNetwork, you will generate both referred and repeat business.

Figure 1.2   Networking Levels Matrix

Level 1 Baseline Networking	Level 2 Strategic Networking	Level 3 Referral Source Networking	Level 4 Mega-Networking
Networking Groups	Industry Niches	Leveraging	Cross-Level Networking
Organization Meetings	Networking Plans	Five-Part Assists	Strategic Alliances
Friends, Relatives	Qualifying Processes	Scheduled Meetings/ Structured Exchanges	Project Collaborations

The MegaNetworking System is useful for everything from one-on-one meetings to more formal networking groups. Chapter 9 details the various types of networking groups. Such groups really can make a difference when you include them in your MegaNetwork plan.

Networking in the '90s

The basic premise of networking is sound, but it has to be taken to another level in the competitive climate of the '90s. Opportunities to build from baseline networking to strategic alliances are shown in the accompanying matrix. These opportunities enable us to move beyond relationships that provide us with information, leads and referral, into what I call the *Big Win.*

When you're working on Level Four, you are leveraging the most you can with your network. By collaborating with others, focusing on *common* rather than *separate* goals, you can accomplish more than either of you could have accomplished individually. The costs are reduced in situations where strategic alliances are present, and the opportunity exists to develop a much broader market. The wins are so strong that all parties involved find themselves appreciating not only the end goal, but the process.

Moving toward a new definition of networking involves looking at going vertical—locating *gold mines*, the best contacts, while avoiding *land mines*, the worst contacts. Each of us has what would be termed a *blind spot*, a place where, although we think we know what's going on, we miss certain things. Having other people who care about us and are aware of the things that matter to us as individuals, we can look out for each other's blind spots. The continuous building of one contact after another is more of a horizontal building of relationships. By going vertical, we are able to find people who begin to understand the motives behind our actions. These people take part and buy into our goals, and we buy into theirs. We begin to understand their needs as they begin to understand ours, often before those needs are even uttered. Our actions begin to speak much louder than our words. We become intuitive individuals, aware in a way that we have never been aware before. We find ourselves able to leverage relationships for one another, creating new leads and referrals easily and effectively.

Learning To Share

There is a big difference between *collaborative* relationship development and the *guerilla growth* strategies used by companies in the '80s. The concept of competition—where each person needed to keep everything they had to themselves in fear of having something taken away—has changed. Now you are encouraged to take something that you have, share it with someone else and end up with something that both of you find useful.

The development of relationships through MegaNetworking enables you to build higher quality circles of influential people where new business opportunities are a constant. No longer will you find the sporadic feast or famine that so many feel when they're out networking.

This book contains my proven system for building a lifetime network of opportunities. It is a system that has worked for thousands of people. While performing my research, I analyzed hundreds of successful networkers. Many of them said that they had grown rich and changed their lives through their ability to network.

Networking is a relationship building process. It is your social self, the person behind the business setting, that creates the foundation for all of your future business and career opportunities. And networking is a skill that you can acquire and cultivate.

Doing It Right

To network effectively, you must be aware of day to day etiquette and strategy. Strategy involves the creation of an action plan to achieve a desired outcome. The goal that everyone wants to achieve is to do more in less time without incurring additional stress. A strategy will help achieve such a goal, but only a life-long system will ensure that the goal is maintained.

MegaNetworking is a lifelong system that provides an ongoing series of strategies that will enable you to start and build a network of powerful, influential relationships. What have you got to lose? Clean out your overstuffed Rolodex, and get ready to make your connections count!

There's a System to MegaNetworking

In his discussions of peak performance, Zig Ziglar differentiates between "doing things right" and "doing the right things." Efficiency involves doing things right, but you can achieve much better results by being effective—doing the right things. With MegaNetworking, you can do the right things by learning some basic rules and applying them to help you get the best payoff for your new prospect development efforts.

Prospecting for Life

Prospecting for new customers or clients can be the most costly, time-intensive activity you perform. However, if done effectively, your prospecting can result in a lifetime of continuous referrals.

Figure 2.1 Networking Levels Matrix			
Level 1 Baseline Networking	**Level 2** Strategic Networking	**Level 3** Referral Source Networking	**Level 4** Mega- Networking
Networking Groups	Industry Niches	Leveraging	Cross-Level Networking
Organiza- tion Meet- ings	Networking Plans	Five-Part Assists	Strategic Alliances
Friends, Relatives	Qualifying Processes	Scheduled Meetings/ Structured Exchanges	Project Collabora- tions

Target the Top

Most networkers set their sights too low, settling for baseline networking activities when they should be using top-level ones (see the above matrix). It's important to focus on industry influencers and referral sources rather than general contacts. Your strategic approach will exponentially yield better and better results. As you sell to these referred prospects, you realize faster and more productive gain. You cut down on your sales or job seeking time because your prospects are predisposed to buying from you. Additionally, your prospects most likely have value systems and attributes similar to your referral source. Starting with your first source, you have the opportunity to build an endless stream of referral sources.

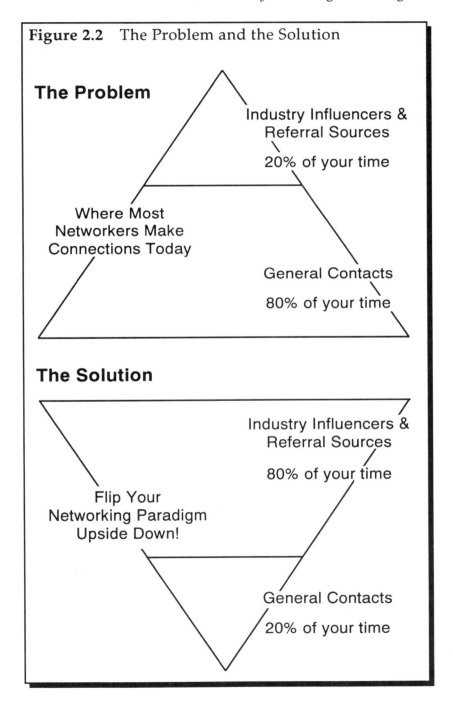

Figure 2.2   The Problem and the Solution

The Problem

Industry Influencers &
Referral Sources

20% of your time

Where Most
Networkers Make
Connections Today

General Contacts

80% of your time

The Solution

Industry Influencers &
Referral Sources

80% of your time

Flip Your
Networking Paradigm
Upside Down!

General Contacts

20% of your time

Building Bases

The number one way that any business grows is through referrals, and most of those referrals come from *internal* sources of referrals—current clients and customers. However, this same result can be achieved by building a base of *external* referral sources. The trick is to first, *identify*, and second, *nurture* relationships with these external sources.

The next step in building an effective network is to identify the base of contacts that could turn into the best external sources. The key is further identifying *influencers*.

Influencers

An influencer is anyone who has leverage with others you wish to prospect. Notice I didn't say that the influencer has to have current influence with others, just the *potential* to influence is the key. Influencers in your target markets are those who can influence others to use your service or product or employ you. They can be anyone—from family members to friends to new acquaintances—in your personal or professional life. They are supporters of others. They view the world as a gigantic two-way street.

Christine Harvey is this kind of networker. Having built a successful career as a consultant to Fortune 500 companies, Christine found herself with the rare opportunity to relocate her business to Europe. She centered her firm in London and began developing relationships through the London Chamber of Commerce. Christine volunteered her time on committees and focused on supporting the efforts of small businesses in London. Christine says that it was this sincere effort to support the Chamber's efforts and her focus on policy issues that helped her achieve a position as the first woman chairperson for the London Chamber of Commerce.

It takes both an interest and a proactive attitude to influence. Someone who is interested in you, not necessarily in what you do, is a prime candidate for becoming an influencer. Influencers are anyone anywhere—from secretaries to CEOs; from the doorman to the person you sit next to on the train.

Sales consultant Jim Pullano had the good fortune of finding a great influencer during one of his sales calls. When Jim found that his appointment with the owner of a company would be delayed, he took the time to chat with the receptionist at the front desk. After 20 minutes of casual conversation, Jim asked, "Tell me, Sandra, who do you know really well here?"

Sandra smiled and said, "Well, the person I know best is the CEO. His wife and I have a common interest in collecting antiques. My husband and I and Mr. and Mrs. Kramer often spend our Saturdays hunting for antiques." Throughout the conversation Jim made notes of the connections Sandra had created with the CEO. He was able to later leverage that influence by building a relationship with Sandra.

When Jim got back to the office after his sales call with Mr. Kramer, he sent both Sandra and Mr. Kramer thank you cards. To this day, Jim maintains a strong relationship with Sandra. When he calls, he always chats with her first. Sandra reports on what's been happening at the company recently and even what kind of mood Mr. Kramer is in before Jim talks with him! Also, knowing some of Mr. Kramer's personal interests, Jim has sent him notices of upcoming auctions. These are the actions that help grow the roots of the relationship deeper.

Some influencers are very visible. You may read about them in the paper or hear them speak at seminars and association meetings. They're the people who are mentioned most frequently in conversations regarding a particular industry. Regis McKenna, one of this country's leading marketing experts, refers to these people as *industry influencers*, because they are the experts in any given industry—the 10 percent that influence the other 90 percent. Subtle influencers like Sandra and more visible ones like speakers at seminars both demonstrate the validity of the Pareto Principle.

By focusing on influencers, you can identify the people who best match your personalities and interests—proactive networkers, willing to become referral sources. The development of these relationships will accomplish two goals They will provide you with a continuous source of new business opportunities, and reduce your time, efforts and stress levels. The second result is actually more important, because when you look at the bigger picture of your life, you begin to realize (if you haven't done so already) that after a while, you will come to a crossroad.

You've worked very hard and might be among those who have achieved substantial recognition, satisfaction and wealth. Yet, at some point you find yourself wondering about the quality of your life. MegaNetworking focuses on that quality. Your relationships are rewarding—personally as well as financially—if you focus on one other key element of a good referral source.

Center Your Relationships on Your Values

It took me a long time to realize that if I began a relationship with a referral source founded with shared values, I would be doing myself the best favor I could imagine. Whereas our interests change throughout our lives, our values tend to remain much the same as when we were children. Of course, there are instances of people who make dramatic changes either for the better or the worse. For the most part, however, we hang on to the values we developed at about age five. Consider Robert

Fulghum's best selling book, *All I Really Need To Know I Learned in Kindergarten.* Fulghum was drawing our attention to the creation of a lifelong value system.

What came as a surprise to me was that if I had asked myself the question—"Does this person have values similar to those I hold dear?"—I could have spared myself months or years of pain. I'm sure that we've all experienced relationships that we thought were wonderful because the other party had similar interests. Or perhaps we maintain relationships with people because we need their help. But when we later reflect on those relationships, we find that the other party didn't hold the same values. I often tell people in my talks to "listen with your eyes." If what people *say* and what they *do* are consistently different, be concerned. Focus your attention on others who "walk their talk," as Dr. Steven Covey points out in his best-selling book, *The 7 Habits of Highly Effective People.*

In his study of value systems, Covey recommends that we focus on our "Circle of Influence" rather than our "Circle of Concern." Referring to the daily matters we address in our lives, Covey emphasizes that as we continually pay attention to what or whom we can influence, our concerns diminish.

The key to MegaNetworking is to focus on what you can create with others. Take the time up front to decide if you and a referral source hold similar values. You want to work with people who understand your values and are interested in doing business based upon the values you share. The awareness of beginning and building from a base of shared values will create an atmosphere of trust and mutual respect.

Learning To Exchange

When both parties are committed to sharing resources, you can build a long-term relationship that is proactive rather than reactive. Together you will exchange new business and career opportunities more easily. Eventually, the exchange will become a positive habit for both parties. You can achieve twice the results of traditional networking in half the time because you have a system of exchange that is continuous. Unlike traditional networking, you won't have to resell yourself to new contacts on a daily basis. You can get to almost anyone you want to meet by being introduced from one referred source to another. You meet people who are *predisposed* to helping you in some way. The first step in the process is to identify a base of referral sources with common values.

Meeting Your Referral Sources

In Chapter 3 you will find information on the first step in building a MegaNetwork—reviewing your existing base of contacts. This step is required to better identify those who would make good referral sources. Chapter 4 takes you to the next step—developing a base of referral sources. There are some simple strategies for finding referral sources that I will preview here.

Start by targeting the industries where you are interested in building relationships. Second, research those industries through key industry publications and by talking with people at associations. Always use the strategy of approaching people whose judgment you most value, asking them which publications and organizations are the best. Continue to ask these questions of the people you meet further into your search. By starting and building through recommendations of those people, patterns will emerge. Eventually, you will be able to differentiate between those in the know and those who are less aware. Keep a list of those who have a particular knack for assessment and discernment. They are wonderful sources for future marketing information. Next, rank your list of industry influencers on a scale of one to five, with one being minimal influence into their targeted industries and five being maximum influence.

The next step is to develop a strategy for introducing yourself, or being introduced, to a referral source. Make it a habit to stay informed of any opportunity to meet face-to-face with industry influencers. Attend talks and workshops where you can meet them. A successful strategy is to sit up front during a presentation. Be prepared by jotting down a point of interest you heard on the back of your business card. After the presentation, approach the presenter to introduce yourself and discuss the point you've noted—if there is not a line of people standing behind you.

The goal is to get the speaker to acknowledge you, to realize your interest in his or her topic and to make a connection—a point of shared interest—for future conversation. In keeping with this goal, hand the speaker your card and ask for one in return. Finally, ask if you may call to discuss the topic further. This is how I met a great referral source and friend, Jeri Sedlar. Jeri, co-author of *On Target*, was one of the first people to help me realize that I was settling for less when I could create so much more.

Jeri was giving a talk at a large conference in Springfield, Illinois. I had traveled there with another consultant who was also a speaker. After listening to Jeri's powerful keynote speech during the awards luncheon, I decided to stop waiting for people to come to me. I went up front, introduced myself and handed Jeri my card. I found out that although she was a past editor of *Working Woman* magazine, she was a recent start-up entrepreneur. When I offered her assistance in growing her consulting business, she seemed very pleased and asked me to call her in New York. About two weeks later, I called.

Jeri was very warm and receptive, remembering who I was and how I had offered to help her. I gave her some general tips and then shared some insights on what I had learned running a business for six years. We concluded our conversation with an agreement to talk at least once a month. Two years later, I still talk with Jeri once a month. We have become good friends and continuous supporters of each other.

I have learned two very important things from our relationship. First, keeping in contact with someone who is not in your local area is actually easier. Why? Because there isn't such a strong expectation that you should be calling more often. You also get more information exchanged in a shorter time because you value the fact that the person calling is spending much more money calling long distance than locally. (I have tested this theory out many times, and it has yet to fail me.)

Second, I found that I had more local connections here than Jeri does. Therefore, I was more aware of the groups that might want to have Jeri speak. Once I located several opportunities, I began using Jeri's name as leverage to build good attendance at the organizations with which I was affiliated. In fact, I just helped my firm start what we called our first Executive Women's Roundtable and used Jeri as the speaker on balancing personal and professional lives. We had a great turnout and wonderful feedback. In turn, Jeri secured an important new piece of business from one of the attendees!

Be Considerate of Time

Some people don't feel comfortable talking to people they perceive to have more influence than they do. I have found, however, that most speakers (and writers) will talk to people who have seen them or read about them and appreciate what they have presented. The key is to be genuinely interested and considerate of other people's time.

If the contacts you meet are open to calls, always ask when it would be most convenient for you to call them. Next, emphasize that you will only call for five or ten minutes at most. When you call, remind your contact of this self-imposed time limit. Keep to your prearranged time limit so that when you ask if you can call again, you will most likely find someone who is quite receptive. Respecting someone's time works because none of us has enough of it. Time is the one commodity that we can't get more of once it's gone. Therefore, if you value someone's time, you are valuing something extremely important to them. They will appreciate you and show that appreciation by allowing another phone appointment, providing you with inside information about your market and promoting you to those in your industry. You have the unlimited potential to develop a much deeper, long-lasting relationship.

Make No Small Plans

Make big plans for contacting key industry influencers. Why plan? When you plan you become more proactive under stress and manage conflict more effectively, which further ensures optimization of time. When you plan you also build commitment to yourself, especially when you put things in writing.

You become even more motivated and committed as you see yourself meeting the goals you have set. It is often said that there is no stronger motivator than success. Just remember to set realistic goals. A goal that is unrealistic is more of a wish. A good strategy is to begin by setting smaller goals that realize some quick successes. These successes can then be used as the foundation for continuous improvement. An example of some goals that are easily achieved might be contacting five new people a week to develop one referral relationship within a month.

Lateral Thinking

Also, take time to ponder the moment. Get in touch with your thoughts, organizing them to more easily address your best modus operandi. Edward de Bono's book, *Serious Creativity*, focuses on using lateral thinking to create the best plan for your goals. Lateral thinking is the process of looking beyond your current base of awareness, drawing attention to the potential. For example, let's say you want to become a very successful business owner in less time and with less effort than it is taking others. You could choose the approach used by Doug Mellinger, owner of Platform Re-engineering Technology Corporation of America (PRT). Mellinger targeted the 30 most powerful chief information officers in the computer industry to be his mentors. They assisted him in the process of building his own successful computer business, and Mellinger found himself the happy recipient of years of collective wisdom. In four years, after starting with only $12,000, Mellinger is the proud owner of a company bringing in around $10 million in sales.

Goal Setting

In order to achieve the kind of success you have in mind—whatever your definition may be—you need to begin by setting goals, creating a plan and taking action to achieve those goals. Your goals may change, but your broader vision of the kind of life you want to have will remain rather stable. By staying flexible and allowing better goals to replace those you have achieved or no longer desire, you will constantly uncover new opportunities.

Start by creating a plan that includes four phases.

Figure 2.3   The Four Phase Plan

	Goal	Action
Planning	Create a vision of what is possible today, three months, six months and one year from today.	Sketch an outline. Identify hurdles. Incorporate evaluation measures.
Explore a path or two.	Take a small step.	For example, call one person you haven't spoken with in a while who really appreciates you and your work, or go alone or with a friend to a meeting of an organization that you have been wanting to go to for a while.
Initiate an action plan.	Keep to your plan at least 80% of the time. You will be integrating your new behavior into your old, so you will find yourself in a phase of adjustment. It won't feel comfortable at first, but sooner than later (21 days) you will become comfortable and be able to build on your new behavior	
Reflect and readjust.	Continuously improve what is working. Eliminate those things that don't work for you. Include both successes and challenges	Ponder. Journal.

Target the companies you would like to work with, and pinpoint prospects or decision makers and other company influencers. Influencers can provide you with valuable information and tips on approaching the prospect that you want to meet. They may even provide you with introductions. Your target group should be the people who have influence with the places where you'd like to do business. These people could be on the outside (suppliers to the company, consultants, colleagues) or on the inside (employees of the company).

Obtain Introductions:
Qualify and Exchange

How do you gain introductions through influential people? First, qualify your contacts based on various factors, such as whether they are proactive (give referrals without being asked, creating opportunities for you) or reactive (must be asked for a referral). Once you have developed a relationship with influential people, you will naturally build bridges of trust that provide a two-way channel of communication. This channel will enable you to ask for introductions without feeling apprehensive.

You will find that your participation in a relationship founded on mutual interest and respect yields ongoing opportunities for growth. You will sometimes ask for things that your sources can't provide. But maintain open communications. Respect your sources for their opinions, and they will respect yours. In an environment of trust, you can feel comfortable in asking, even if you find that you have asked the wrong question or asked it too soon. The candor that develops in a close relationship allows for a more dynamic, fluid exchange. You don't have to worry that you will be misunderstood. With this trust comes the opportunity to challenge each other, and you will both grow as a result. This in turn opens new avenues to benefit your business or career.

When you build rapport up front, establishing a base of referral sources before you need them, you can ask for introductions when you want them. Make asking for introductions a regular part of an ongoing exchange with your referral sources. In upcoming chapters you will be given some useful tools to help you gain referrals and introductions.

Creating Benefits: The Five-Part Assist

When you network effectively, you create a casual yet anticipated exchange. But, you can't exchange if you don't honestly feel that you deserve to be a recipient. By creating structure, you can increase opportunities for continuous leads and referrals. The result is what I referred to earlier as the "Big-Win"—unlimited goal achievement for all parties involved.

Start with *emotional support*. Jean Nidetch, president of multi-million dollar Weight Watchers International, created a company based on strong emotional support. Finding herself at 214 pounds and very dissatisfied, Jean began to seek solace from her friends. It was the emotional support that she shared with others that led Jean to realize the power of this form of exchange. In time, this support became the foundation for Jean's incredible success.

Dale Carnegie once said, "When dealing with people, remember you are not dealing with creatures of logic, but with creatures of emotion." If you find yourself thinking that you don't know what you have to offer someone who is an influencer, you're not alone. Many of the clients I coach have felt the same way. I emphasize to them that they have much more to offer than they think. It all starts with the basics of building relationships, creating *first* an emotional connection.

In essence, you are selling yourself. Successful salespeople everywhere realize that people buy on emotion and justify with fact. Emotional support creates the foundation for all long-lasting relationships. And you best share emotional support when you begin by *appreciating* others.

Appreciating is a very active process. When you appreciate others, you recognize their importance. It involves challenging yourself to be specific about what you perceive to be the value that you are receiving from others and then communicating those thoughts to them.

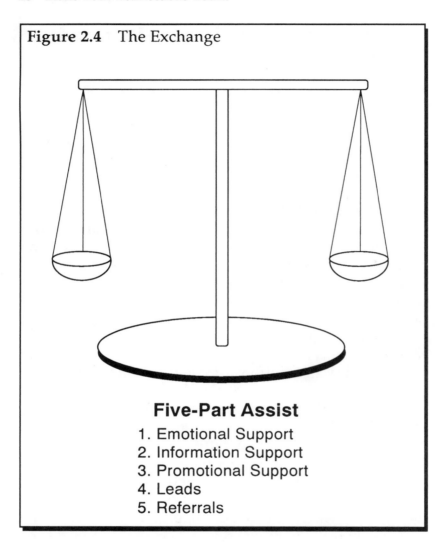

Figure 2.4   The Exchange

Five-Part Assist

1. Emotional Support
2. Information Support
3. Promotional Support
4. Leads
5. Referrals

This can be anything from complimenting the way someone dresses, to discussing the statements they make or noting the actions they have taken.

For example, if I have heard something good about someone, I take the opportunity to mention it to them. People may act humble when you compliment them, but it is likely that they will appreciate your interest in their lives.

Above all else, remember that at the core of appreciation is genuineness—a sincere respect and interest in others.

Once you make an emotional connection, you have set the stage for an exchange of information. *Information support* is any kind of information—surveys, articles, upcoming seminars etc., that would be helpful to your sources. By looking for information to help your sources build an awareness of their market, you can save them time, money and frustration. It's like having the finest market research firm provide you with timely insider information on a continuous basis. We all have blind spots—places within our conscious minds where gaps of awareness or understanding exist. The exchange of information support addresses the importance of constantly updating our knowledge base.

I regularly receive articles on networking and notes from referral sources apprising me of upcoming events focused on the subject. By educating your sources as to one or two areas of interest to you and then initiating an information exchange, you will later find yourself the recipient of this strategy.

As our exchanges develop, we naturally begin to tell others about the people making a difference in our lives. This is the third assist, *promotional support.* By recognizing this powerful marketing strategy, you can dramatically increase your name recognition and new business opportunities. Eventually, you will find yourself meeting people you have never met before who say, "I've heard of you. So and so told me some great things about you!" This third-party endorsement builds crediblity and trust faster than any other form of marketing. Once trust is developed you can spend more time on matching your skills to the potential new business or career opportunities that this assist has created. In other words, people who have heard favorable things about you *before* meeting you will be *predisposed* to buying from you, hiring you or referring you to others. Very often, those who are good at getting endorsements are more aware of the *system* of finding and nurturing these sources. The basics lie in implementing the MegaNetworking System presented in this book. You can expect an increase in new business and career opportunities as you begin to use the system on a daily basis.

The fourth assist is the use of *leads*—pieces of information about potential prospects where there is no current relationship developed by your source. Leads are a natural result of information gathering. By being aware of your source's needs, you will naturally identify opportunities that your source can further pursue. Leads are quite different from referrals—leads are nonqualified contact names, while referrals include a direct contact and a recommendation.

Referrals, the fifth assist, are the brass ring. You want them, but don't expect them in the initial stages of a relationship. Instead, your primary focus should be on building a solid relationship through the first four assists that lead to referrals.

Now that you understand the Five-Part Assist—emotional support, promotional support, information support, leads and referrals, challenge yourself. A certain amount of dissatisfaction can be very healthy. When you are dissatisfied, you eventually break through to a new level, choosing what you want to do to replace what you are no longer happy doing.

For Vicki Spina, dissatisfaction meant a new career focus and pursuing her dream. Vicki wanted more control over her life; she also wanted to write. After a number of years as a top sales producer in the area of executive search, Vicki went on to write a book on the top strategies for getting hired in today's competitive environment. When Vicki didn't receive an offer to publish her book, she decided to publish it herself. Entering the world of self-publishing meant a tremendous time and dollar commitment. Vicki also needed to learn the ins and outs of the publishing industry. Only a small percentage of self-published books is ever considered for mass distribution in bookstores. Vicki challenged herself, however, not only to get her books into major bookstore chains, but to become nationally known as a speaker and consultant.

Vicki accomplished all three of her goals. Today, after only one year in publication, Vicki's book, *Getting Hired in the '90s,* has sold more than 11,000 copies. Waiting in the wings are offers to purchase Vicki's books as premium items for graduating college students. Orders are beginning to roll in for purchases of 10,000-50,000 books at one time. At a time when the average book sells 3,000 copies, Vicki's accomplishment reminds us that a certain amount of dissatisfaction can be the catalyst that turns pessimism into prosperity.

One final word on the Five-Part Assist. Initially, your focus should be on gathering information and building trust through emotional support. You can do this by offering information that you have already gathered or doing some simple homework to acquire one or two pieces of information that would be of interest to your source. Once you develop credibility, you can ask for introductions.

Review and Readjust

MegaNetworkers never sit on their contacts like misers hoarding gold. Instead, they are constantly evaluating who they know, determining what leads are worth keeping and what leads no longer meet their needs.

Many people put all their energy into planning, forgetting that the real growth takes place *after* the plan has been developed. As you implement your plan, commit to weekly reviews. You will find that once implemented, some things work better than others. Keep evaluating the effectiveness of your efforts. Develop your own system from the suggestions contained in this book.

The Six-Step System To
Building Your Own MegaNetwork

In the following chapters you will learn the six steps to creating a MegaNetwork. Here is an overview:

1. **Lay the groundwork.**   Learn how to analyze your current base of contacts to determine who would be best suited for an ongoing exchange.

2. **Build your base of referral sources**.   Identify influencers in your target market as well as in other markets. These sources will be the base of ongoing support and referrals.

3. **Create winning first impressions.**   Take an interest in others first. Learn what it takes to get people to take an interest in you and/or your business or career.

4. **Master the exchange.**   Discover how to use the tools that will make all your exchanges more productive. Now you can get the results you want *when* you want them.

5. **Leverage your best sources of influence.**   Once you've built your base, you need to build your MegaNetwork. Learn the science of leveraging and creating opportunities for unlimited referrals.

6. **Manage the four levels of networking.**   Organize and prioritize your efforts to achieve maximum results. Reduce stress as you gain control over your goals.

Your focus should be on the people who can help you take advantage of opportunities, rather than on the opportunities themselves.

"In the '80s your network was your pipeline to opportunities. In the '90s it will be your lifeline," says Jeri Sedlar. Together we can achieve so much more. Three to six months of building a base of quality relationships can be done easily and almost effortlessly if we just take time to start today.

The introduction is the beginning. The process of staying connected, "co-creating" opportunities with others following an initial meeting, is what MegaNetworking is all about. Don't be afraid that you don't have anything to offer today. You don't need to:

- have an in-depth knowledge of another's industry;
- have any current leads or referrals to give;
- have to manipulate the conversation to get the other party to focus on your needs;
- have to feel as though you are pushy; or
- have to offer anything more than appreciation for the other person.

Match Where You're At

Last year I acquired a client who was very charming. I enjoyed working with him to grow his business. We both could benefit from his success as a trainer. The work I was doing went smoothly until I started to work with his partner. The partner, I found, was nothing like my original client. This partner was rude, constantly interrupting me and failing to listen when I suggested project changes. It was not long before I told my client that he would need to find someone else to work with his firm. From that day forward I chose to look for clients who held values and attitudes similar to mine.

Today, the firm I work at has promoted this strategy, which has evolved into locating clients who have attitudes that "match where we're at." We are looking for the "success attitude." Companies that nurture this attitude have the ability to grow as big as they desire. They are involved in continuous quality improvement (CQI) and total quality management (TQM). They offer my firm the opportunity to build relationships that last for a lifetime.

Success begins with you. Start by respecting yourself, recognizing that you have much to offer. As Leo Buscaglia emphasizes in his book, *Living, Loving & Learning*, in order to develop self-respect, we should focus not only on our *actuality*, but on our *potentiality*. Buscaglia encourages people to create bridges of communication—strong bridges that will withstand obstacles and gaps.

Start by finding out who you are today and consider your potential. To do this you need to first identify what I call your *emotional truths*. Remember, people buy on emotion and justify with facts. You will create your strongest and longest networking relationships when you hold shared emotional truths with another.

For example, you might be a tax accountant who loves to save people money at tax time. You share a truth with others who love saving people money. These people might be your clients, your contacts—or both. They respect you.

Respect is one of the key words in a long-term exchange. It is the foundation you lay to build your communication bridge. As Buscaglia emphasizes, "It all starts with you."

Make a commitment to respect your work. How? By doing whatever you can to appreciate everything you do. Each time you take a step to develop your base of referral sources, congratulate yourself. Realize that the investment you make in these early relationships will be more worthwhile than almost any you will make within your lifetime. You are building your emotional (first) and financial (second) security through these relationships. Later, you will have the opportunity to enjoy the great fruits of your labor. Therefore, take the time now to build your base.

For the first time, networking is presented in this book as a purposeful and systematic discipline. Further, it is a science rather than an art. This is because at its foundation, the abilities necessary to build successful relationships that are mutually beneficial are skills rather than inherent talents. MegaNetworking enables you to take advantage of something that already exists—your current connections, your relationships. Through these connections you create tributaries to anyone you want to meet. Using the MegaNetworking System, you can access intended prospects as well as those who are presented by your referral sources and contacts.

Work through the exercises that are interspersed throughout this book. They will help you quickly integrate the MegaNetworking System into your current work life.

Remember, it's not your referral sources who will be your ultimate focus, but the hidden network of prospects *behind* those sources. The most important skill to learn in networking is the skill of exchanging. You give something of value in anticipation of something of equal or greater value. You continuously work to educate your referral sources so that they are thoroughly aware of your interests and needs. It is in these ongoing exchanges that we realize the potential of MegaNetworking—the ability to *create*. When we exchange in an environment of trust and interest, we are free to create connections that have maximum benefit for both parties.

Future chapters will focus on the exchange and its various components. You will find that you have much to offer, and in turn, much will be offered to you. Travel through these chapters with an open mind, and enjoy.

3

Step 1:
Laying the
Groundwork

Remember when Mark Twain's Tom Sawyer was told by Aunt Polly that he had to whitewash the picket fence? Clever Tom was successful in manipulating a crowd of playmates into actually *wanting* to whitewash the fence. He accomplished this feat by pretending to enjoy painting so much that his friends began to request the chance to work. When Tom's friends clamored to take their turn at painting, Tom even acted reluctant to let anyone else take away his pleasure.

Leveraging Your Contacts

Why was Tom so successful? He *knew* what motivated others. He knew that people want what satisfies their emotional needs. Here, Tom's playmates wanted to be part of the fun. If something (the fence) was supposed to be more fun than play, Tom's friends certainly wanted to participate. In other words, the perceived benefits of painting were each child's current reality. As one child after another got the chance to paint, the other children wanted to paint even more.

The emotional fervor that Tom was able to create is similar to the potential that you have for building a base of referral sources, once others see your pleasure at building relationships. Unlike Tom, though, you will not have to manipulate people to get them to help you. Rather you seek to *leverage* the connections of each contact.

Greek mathematician and physicist, Archimedes, once said that he could move the whole world if he just had a lever that was long enough. In networking, your success will grow as you build the skills necessary to *leverage* relationships by creating a strong, supportive network of contacts. In turn, as these contacts develop into referral sources, they will become the foundation of your MegaNetwork, ultimately leading to many new business opportunities.

Leveraging doesn't involve manipulation; it involves influence and power. The goal in MegaNetworking is to produce relationships that offer the maximum benefits to all parties involved. Leveraging is the process necessary to create such a network. It involves first, identifying the contacts that currently offer the strongest potential to exchange via the Five-Part Assist (emotional, promotional and information support, leads and referrals) and setting up meetings (either in person or by phone) to generate ongoing assists.

I've gotten additional business, either directly or indirectly, from people I've met on airplanes, on elevators, in restaurants, on vacation, through telemarketing surveys, through causes I support and through those who are in businesses similar to mine.

Figure 3.1 Your Current Contacts—Who Is Your Network?

Alan Simmons, CSP, The Simmons Group in Ontario, Canada, uses the chart below to identify his current network:

Accountant	Government	Phone Company
Airlines	Departments	Printer
Auto Sales	Grocery Store	Real Estate
Banker	Insurance	Agent
Cable TV	Agents	Relatives
Coffee Shop	Lawyer	Restaurants
Computers	Librarian	Service Station
Courier	Mechanic	Speakers
Dentist	Neighbors	Taxi Company
Doctor	Office Supplies	Travel Agent
Dry Cleaner	Past	Utility
Gas Company	Employers	Video Store

Alan was able to generate 350 warm contacts from this list.

It's Not Who You Know, but Who You Get To Know

Next, focus on the hidden network behind each contact. All of these contacts will have some degree of influence. During exchanges you will learn:

- who is currently in your contact's network;
- what kind of people these prospects interact with regularly;
- who the prospects' suppliers and customers are;
- what organizations the prospects belong to; and

Figure 3.2   Who Can You Currently Influence?

Take five minutes to write down all the people with whom you currently have influence. Rank the degree of this influence for each person on a scale of one to five, with one being a low degree of influence and five being a very high degree.

Name Address	Phone Rank	Comment
_____	(___)_____	_____
_____	_____	_____
_____	(___)_____	_____
_____	_____	_____
_____	(___)_____	_____
_____	_____	_____
_____	(___)_____	_____
_____	_____	_____
_____	(___)_____	_____
_____	_____	_____
_____	(___)_____	_____
_____	_____	_____

The beauty of networking is its ever-expanding, changing nature—the evolution of people connecting people to new contacts, no matter what their organizational affiliation. Even if you have just moved to a new area, you probably have the beginnings of a network that can be cultivated and expanded over time. If you are well established, you may have an enormous number of people in your life with whom you can continually exchange referrals and information.

- the degree of influence these prospects have with others.

After creating a list of these people:

- Put an "R" next to the names of those you network with regularly and an "S" next to the names of those you interact with sporadically.
- Rank the prospects from one to five, placing the fives at the top of your list.
- Choose the prospects who might be referral sources—see Chapter 4.
- Keep a separate sheet on those you could give business to and those who would bring you the most business.
- If you have a situation where you or the other party can't reciprocate equally, talk about a different form of remuneration—e.g., mailing lists, product or service exchange, etc. Negotiate an equal exchange.

Once you have a list of people with whom you currently have the strongest influence, take another look. Use Figure 3.3 on page 42 to separate the givers from the takers.

Know What Makes You Tick

In order to create the foundation for a base of sources and repeat referral opportunities that will last a lifetime, you must begin by analyzing yourself. Find out what makes you tick.

When we talk about what makes us tick, there are a couple of things involved. First, what's really important to you? Is it yourself, your family, the things that you can acquire in life? Is it your spiritual devotion? Now, all of these things might be important to you, but if you could draw a pie and put down which areas represent what percentage of what matters to you, how would that pie look?

Figure 3.3   Givers or Takers?

Givers	Takers
1. Ask questions about you. For example: What do you do that you enjoy the most?	1. Ask questions that benefit them, never about you. For example: What do you do that can help me?
2. Think of an equal exchange of support— information, leads, referrals.	2. Constantly ask for help getting business.
3. Spend the majority of time listening and asking yourself questions about you and your needs.	3. Talk about themselves constantly.
4. Keep a rather steady gaze into your eyes. Show a sincere interest in you.	4. Often look though you or have roving eyes. For example: If you are at a gathering, they might keep looking around for the next party to meet.
5. Smile sincerely. Their eyes match their mouths.	5. Smile, but insincerely. Their eyes don't match their mouths.
6. Stay in contact with you.	6. Only call you when they need something from you.
7. Return calls promptly.	7. Return calls when it suits them, if at all.

I find that creating some type of visual representation of where you spend your time helps you focus on what really matters to you today. This exercise also helps you discover that certain areas of your life, at this time, aren't that important. As you draw this pie, you will find that there are areas that are very important. What you are looking for are not only things that you find interesting, but areas that you might not be developing right now that you may want to develop in the future. These areas represent bridges that will create opportunities for you through the efforts of other people. As you recognize what those areas are, you will be more selective as to where to spend your time. However, this will take some time. There is nothing that can replace the quiet time when you can sit down and figure out what's right for you.

Once you've drawn your pie, write down the activities that you are most skilled at and which you most enjoy. Second, list the skills that you would like to create or develop. Where can you go or whom can you ask to assist you in skill creation and improvement? Are there courses or seminars that you can attend?

You might say, "There is no time to plan." However, you must *make time to plan*. What I find useful is to make time one day a week for planning. Keep a journal. Get one that appeals to you, such as a blank-lined hard cover book. What you find over time is that there's a pattern to your learning. You begin to unearth the things that really do matter to you—the things you are proud of achieving and the things that you long to achieve. This strategy is also very useful for discovering the things that don't really matter to you.

If you have trouble finding out what does matter to you, I recommend starting with the things that you don't want to do. When you have completed the first step of finding what you enjoy doing, what does matter to you, then take a very realistic look at your strengths—developed skills and areas of improvement—underdeveloped

---

Figure 3.4   Underdeveloped or Undeveloped Skills

An Example:

1. _Creating financial projections_____

2. _Writing fiction_____

3. _Learning a foreign language_____

Underdeveloped or Undeveloped Skills

Your Turn

1. _____

2. _____

3. _____

---

or undeveloped skills. Rather than areas of weakness, I choose to call them areas of improvement, because there are very few areas that, if focused on over a period of time, won't become stronger. In Figure 3.4 above, identify three undeveloped skills that you would like to develop.

On the Receiving End

Because networking is the result of people building relationships with one another, the terms networking and network are often misleading. Networking is not something that you have to work at. Networking involves being receptive to others who are interested in working with you to help you build your new business opportunities.

Problems most often arise, surprisingly, from a fear of disclosing your inner self. For instance, it is often difficult to allow yourself to be vulnerable when building relationships. There is a natural fear of being rejected, being taken advantage of or discovering that a contact you've made doesn't fit your idea of a good networker.

All relationships are dynamic, however, constantly changing in makeup. Through your proactive attitude, your relationships can be altered or minimized so that your focus is on those who can provide you with more of an equal exchange. That's where MegaNetworking enters the picture.

Locate individuals who have complementary strengths and skills. Additionally, people who work in a field complementary to yours are more often in a position to refer you because your skills, products or services may be needed after theirs. For instance, if you are an architect or in the architectural field, you would benefit from building a primary network comprised of referral sources in the fields of telecommunications, commercial moving and real estate. Here, the natural flow of referrals may start with the real estate professional who, upon obtaining a client looking to move, refers the architectural firm, who in turn refers the telecomunications firm, who in turn refers the moving company!

Finding these people requires planning time. Additionally, this activity is something that you will be doing on an ongoing basis. In the beginning, you are just looking for one or two people who fit this criteria. You can ease stress by acknowledging that this is not about finding dozens and dozens of people who can provide you with leads and referrals. Rather, this is about finding one or two people who, within a short period of time, will end up providing you with a continuous stream of *quality* referrals.

How Do You Know Them?

In determining the level of influence that your current contacts have with others, start by ranking their *degree of influence*. The degree of influence can be determined by the level of interest your contact shows in staying in touch with others and being proactive. Calling other people, finding out what they've been up to and *who* they've been keeping in touch with is essential. By developing this information about your contacts, you can determine whether they are appropriate referral sources.

Remember, a referral source will be someone whom you can look to for constant connections over the long-term instead of a contact who might sporadically provide you with connections over the short-term.

Another indicator in determining whether someone is a referral source involves assessing his or her degree of interest in a continuous exchange. Obviously, if someone is interested in finding others themselves, there is a much higher level of commitment to an exchange.

There is also the question of how well you know the contact. This can be a matter of discovering whether the contact is someone you know you can count on for the long run versus someone who appears to be interested in an exchange but is primarily interested in providing for themselves. Seek a *we* rather than a *me* exchange. There must be a mutual benefit to networking.

Find out the answers to these kinds of questions by asking what type of information your contacts are interested in exchanging. If they're only focused on leads and referrals, then the exchange will be one-sided. Avoid those who see the process as an opportunity to take as much as possible and then move on. You will know these people by the way they handle themselves during your structured exchanges. They will constantly change the conversation to address their needs.

For example, someone who is focused on an equal exchange will keep asking, "What can I do for you?" These people will operate at a higher level of communication with you. They are interested in your success. They ask about your recent achievements almost every time they see you. Tell them good news; they are genuinely pleased for you. Equal exchangers don't rush the conversation or constantly refocus it on themselves. They are interested in finding out about you and what makes you successful. They also share what has worked well for them.

Stick with Those Who Share

One networker told me that he was extremely disappointed with the referral sources he had been connecting with lately. They were people who were only interested in him because he had just left a large corporation and wanted to tap into his contacts. They were more interested in finding out whom he knew than in offering him any help. Remember, when you do find a good referral source, that person is worth more than all the contacts you could possibly gather. Therefore, make sure that you rearrange your schedule to spend your time with the sharers, leaving no time for the takers.

In *Networking Smart*, Wayne Baker says that the average person has approximately 3,500 contacts. When we're looking at ranking, 3,500 contacts might be the number of people we meet, but that is a far cry from the number of people with whom we have a high level of influence. When ranking influence, use a scale between one and five. Look for at least one five—someone who has a very high degree of influence with others and is willing to be proactive and look for new opportunities for you without being asked.

The extra bonus is that these types of people will be with you for the long term. Six months, one year, two years from now, they will still be out looking for new opportunities for you. They will also show you how best to help them. Remember, the exchange is more of a process of *qualifying* and assisting each other.

Added Benefits

I find that a number of people have a network they rely on for providing them with leads and referrals. But they quickly forget all of the other benefits of having a network. For example, by working your network, you can develop relationships to a point where you are collaborating on projects and creating strategic alliances with other organizations and larger companies.

Your goal is to build the best network possible. By withholding judgment while you take the time to develop a relationship with the people you've ranked the highest, you will have a more accurate assessment of who will make good sources for the long term. You will have a good base to make this assessment after three face-to-face meetings.

You're on a path now that is dramatically different from the path that you took before. Realize that your choices also will be different. As you continue down this new road, you will find people who will assist you in the process of building relationships for a lifetime. Therefore, you need not be concerned about how many people you're currently meeting. Very likely, during the next three months, you will find yourself feeling a bit overwhelmed. Relax, that is only a temporary feeling.

If you're like many people networking today, you may be experiencing the problem I mentioned earlier of the "overstuffed Rolodex." What do you do with all of those contacts? How do you manage them? Whom do you need to "weed out"?

Finding Effective People

In building a base of referral sources, you're looking for *effective* people who are:

- results-focused—not problem-focused;
- preventive—not reactive;
- value-centered—not self-centered;
- big picture—not detail focused;
- long-term—not short-term.

Effective people are going to be there for you when you need them. They will do whatever it takes to get results. On the other hand, the short-term, reactive, problem-minded people are going to create stress in your life and provide you with much less support.

That's why your values must be the foundation for your networking goals. Here is a sample list of values that many people consider important:

Values

• Honesty	• Empathy
• Integrity	• Intelligence
• Independence	• Follow-Through
• Humor	• Patience
• Perseverance	• Courage
• Ingenuity	• Wisdom
• Quality Performance	• Leadership

If your goals are in conflict with your values or your beliefs, this conflict will be difficult to resolve and will lead to stress. Therefore, you want to find people who have shared values. You will find that those shared values will build a foundation for friendship and support that will last much longer than anything you might currently be experiencing.

Integrity

One of the values most important to me is integrity. Steven Covey tells us that "Integrity is, fundamentally, the value we place on ourselves. It's our ability to make and keep commitments to ourselves, to 'walk our talk.'" In short, actions speak louder than words. Look for others who hold values that you espouse on a daily basis. When you find these people, although they will certainly be in the minority, they will become your lifetime sources, teachers and friends. They will feed you with opportunities, and you will do the same for them.

You will discover that you have a workable network that was not developed from an incredible amount of effort, but rather from a very natural *give-and-take* with other highly-valued people who are strongly motivated to assist you. Of course, there will be upkeep once you develop such a strong network. Through continuous exchanges you will grow a network that will maintain its strength throughout your lifetime.

One Step at a Time

Set aside at least two hours a week to plan your networking. Monday mornings and Friday afternoons are often good times for this.

> "If you clearly define the goal, you are halfway to achieving it"
>
> **Robert Holmes & Court**

> "Studies indicate that 80% of the results you desire will flow from 20% of your activities—especially if those activities involve preparation and relationship building. If you spend 100% of your efforts on managing crises, you will only continue traveling—very efficiently—in the same vicious circle."
>
> **Janet Hauter, *The Smart Woman's Guide to Success***

Figure 3.5 Quality Versus Quantity

Now that you have reflected on the individuals in your current network, take a moment to see your network as a whole. Complete the following exercise to assess the current effectiveness of your network.

I. **Quantity**—Rate today's level of activity with your exchanges on a scale of 1-5 (1 being lowest - 5 being highest).

1. Attending organization meetings to locate new referral sources _____

2. Involving yourself in outside activities (sports, hobbies, religion etc., that involve others) _____

3. Making calls to new contacts to create referral source relationships _____

4. Reading articles to identify influencers and potential referral sources in chosen market niches _____

5. Asking current contacts to recommend potential referral sources _____

6. Spending time planning the development of your referral source base _____

II. **Quality**—Rate today's level of quality with your exchanges on a scale of 1-5 (1 being lowest - 5 being highest).

1. Organization meetings _____

2. Outside activities (sports, hobbies, religious etc., that involve others) _____

3. Contact calls _____

4. Reading articles to identify influencers in chosen market niches and potential referral sources _____

5. Asking current contacts to recommend potential referral sources _____

6. Spending time planning the development of your referral base _____

If you found that your Quality score was lower than your Quantity score, you need to change your focus. A feeling of dissatisfaction can actually be a starting point toward building better networking skills. If you take action to improve your current status, it leads to change.

When you set aside specific time for planning, begin by writing down where you are now. What does your network look like? What is good about it? What would you like to change? If you could have a network that really worked for you, what would it look like? How many referrals would you be receiving weekly, monthly, yearly?

Once you have written these desires out, categorize them. I recommend creating three-month, six-month, ten-month and twelve-month goals. I have found that focusing on these shorter-term goals is much more effective than focusing on a one-year, two-year and three-year plan. It takes at least 21 days to form a new habit; therefore, attention to the short term will enable you to achieve smaller goals that will add up over a year.

Also, track your weekly results. At my firm, we're responsible for filing weekly status reports. Each week I grumble that I have to do it, but remember, those things that are measured have a way of being met. It's easier to get off track when your attention is on some nebulous goal a year away. You need to meet the weekly goals that are tied to your daily activities.

Keep Your Goals Simple

Start by setting just a few new networking goals. For example:

> Goal #1 - Attend one networking event.
>
> Goal #2 - Call some old friends you haven't spoken with lately.

Now, if you meet Goal #1, you can move to Goal #2. Try to keep it simple—everyone is inundated with information. One request made clearly and concisely can create dozens of opportunities.

Not everything comes to us at once—sometimes you have to move to an intermediate idea in order to access, understand or be ready for an idea.

Don't overplan and underact—one form of action would be to learn from other people's actions.

Steps to Laying the Groundwork

- ◆ Remember what's most important to you. Find those things through self-analysis.

- ◆ Analyze your strengths and areas of development in order to create an awareness of who you are, what areas you should be focusing on for future development and what you can offer today.

- ◆ Figure out how you can help others. Create a personal mission statement that indicates what benefits others will receive from buying from you or hiring you.

- ◆ List your accomplishments in one sentence summaries. These will be the basis for developing credibility more quickly with your future referral sources.

- ◆ Look for people with similar values. Your values have been with you much longer than your interests.

- ◆ Rank your contacts—those who have the highest potential for being good referral sources.

- ◆ Focus on the quality, not the quantity, of those with whom you will exchange opportunities.

Step 2:
Building Your Base
of Referral Sources

The strategies described in this chapter will help you create the opportunities that build your base of contacts to generate ongoing referrals. One of the most important things to remember when looking for referral sources is to choose people by their behavior, not so much by their title. People who have a *can-do* proactive attitude can be much better sources than those who are self-focused in positions of strong influence. Therefore, remove any titles that others might have. Don't assume that if someone is the president of an organization he or she will be a good referral source.

Referring Wide and Deep

Referral sources are to the successful entrepreneur and sales professional what a career network of professional associates is to the corporate executive. They are a group of contacts who themselves have networks that reach both wide and deep. Referral sources have built large networks in which they hold influential positions. They offer the opportunity to secure more business than any other marketing strategy you could implement at half the cost. Therefore, it follows that cultivating these people is just as important as traditional sales prospecting. However, very few entrepreneurs have a formal system for tapping into this larger sales development opportunity.

Why? The reason has a great deal to do with the informal structure of networking. Good networkers realize that, although they work with many people, they get the majority of their leads and referrals from a small portion of their contact base. This base usually represents 20 percent of an individual's network.

The Consummate Networker

Bernard Ostrosky is a good example of someone who knows how to utilize his base of referral sources. Bernie, as his friends call him, is an investment broker. He spends at least ten hours a week on the phone networking with people. Others who have had the opportunity to work with Bernie say that he has the "Golden Rolodex." Bernie's *no-pressure* sales approach appeals to many entrepreneurs who are often deluged with people who want to sell them something.

Bernie describes himself as a "conservative investor." "I work best," he says, "with people who want to invest their money over the long term." Bernie spends most of his time finding business for those he calls. He rarely mentions his services—only when the topic moves to investments. In fact, the people who network with Bernie often find themselves asking, "Bernie, what kind of leads or referrals are you looking for?"

At this point, Bernie talks about his skills as an investor. He makes it quite clear that he is not a speculator. He is a conservative investor, preferring to work with people who are interested in conservative investments over a longer term. Those who develop long-term relationships with Bernie have come to respect his requests. Because he is such a strong networker, Bernie has been able to build a very large network of people who would do a great deal for their friend and associate.

Bernie is also very particular about the people he refers to his network. He analyzes their strengths and weaknesses, working them slowly through the various levels of his network, saving the most prestigious leads and referrals for last.

The Six Qualities of Good Referral Sources

First and most importantly, referral sources are *givers*. They enjoy helping others build their businesses. As networking continues to grow into a more structured marketing strategy, you will see more people who have reached certain success points and now look to give something back. One entrepreneur who exemplifies this quality is Pat Biedar. Pat is the owner of a sheet metal fabricating shop in Elk Grove Village, Illinois. Pat, whose company posts more than $6 million in annual revenues, loves to help entrepreneurs.

Pat constantly takes young entrepreneurs under her wing, introducing them at Chamber of Commerce gatherings and other association meetings. Pat plays business matchmaker, locating people she knows in her network who would need what the new entrepreneur has to sell. Pat humbly says that she has had so many people who have helped her become successful that she wants to do something in return. Unexpectedly widowed at the age of 43, Pat took over her husband's company with no prior knowledge of business. She spent many hours learning the basics. Through hard work and perseverance over the past seven years, Pat has converted a company with severe financial problems into a multimillion dollar enterprise.

Sue, another referral source, gave me Pat's name when I was searching for a panelist-speaker for a workshop I was hosting. Sue told me that she would contact. Pat ahead of time so that I would have no trouble getting through to her when I called. Indeed, when I did call, I was immediately connected to Pat. She not only took my call, she accepted my request to speak. We chatted for approximately ten minutes and before the end of the conversation I asked to visit her plant. That request, which' showed an interest in her company, started a reciprocal conversation about my business. This exchange has opened the door for me to network with Pat.

Second, referral sources are *involved in their communities*. It is often mind-boggling to see the number of activities in which these people are involved. Take Mershon Shrigley, owner of an eight-year old marketing firm, for example. Mershon is the chairman of the board of a very successful and active senior center, the program director of a small business department at a local college and active in several local Chambers. In addition, she has started a home-based business networking group. Mershon is an example of a referral source who is committed to developing the businesses in her community.

Third, good referral sources are *aware*, they understand your needs and interests. Such sources take time to listen to the kinds of leads and referrals most beneficial to you. They promise only what they can deliver. They know who would be a good match for your network.

Fourth, good referral sources *take the time to listen*; they intuitively know the type of sources that will benefit you most. There are, of course, people who mean well, but don't understand what kind of referrals are best for you. Think twice about continuing to work with people who will not listen. Explain to the source that your idea of good referrals differs from those you are receiving. If that doesn't work, find another source.

Don't waste time trying to turn a bad referral into a good one. It very seldom works. For example, let's say that you own a computer sales firm and told a referral source that strong referrals for you would include businesses looking to buy new computer systems. You also explained that your target market encompassed companies with at least 20 employees. If the referral source continues to give referrals for companies with less than 20 employees, you need to move on to a new source. Good communication is essential.

You can depend on referral sources to follow through on their word. There is an equal exchange of referrals. These sources sincerely want you to succeed. They see their relationship with you as a *win-win* arrangement. If your sources provide you with profitable referrals, you will reciprocate. There is nothing more useful to your sales growth than a network of referral sources with whom you exchange business opportunities on an ongoing basis.

Fifth, good sources are *persistent*, they continue to work with you through good times and bad. You find these sources interested in more than just one or two networking opportunities. Good sources are genuinely interested in a long-term relationship. They admire you and want to keep in touch no matter what changes might occur in either of your lives.

Sixth, referral sources *share a common vision* with you. While writing my first book, I developed a relationship with Sam McGrier, the regional director of the Small Business Administration (SBA) in my area. Sam knew that my vision was to be a small business advocate, which I accomplished through special entrepreneurial training scholarships for disadvantaged individuals. Sam contacted me every time he knew there was an SBA grant available for teaching entrepreneurs. Through his support and direction, I was able to obtain a development grant to teach a course on networking for entrepreneurs.

Sam's persistent dedication to small business advocacy and to my participation in programs that support this vision has helped me build my company's image and presence in my local community. Sam knows that my plans include future programs offered in other locations throughout the country, and he supports my efforts. In fact, whenever we see one another, Sam makes a point of introducing me to any other government officials who might be present. In turn, I have worked as a volunteer for several SBA conferences in which Sam was involved. He shares my commitment to entrepreneurs and the goals that I have.

Referral sources are everywhere. They have spheres of influence that are constantly growing because the people who influence these networks are constantly nurturing their individual spheres. Places to locate referral sources include:

- Local Chambers of Commerce
- Industry-specific organizations (for example: National Association for Fund Raising Executives)
- *Who's Who* directories
- Speakers at seminars
- Alumni directories (Note the accomplishments of alumni from your university.)
- Business periodicals (look at the column that lists promotions)
- Business magazines (*Business Week, Entrepreneur, Forbes, Fortune, Inc., Nations Business, Newsweek, Success,* etc.)

Figure 4.1 Current Industry Influencers in Your
Target Market

Name & Title   Company
Address   Phone

_____   _____

_____   (____)_____

_____   _____

_____   (____)_____

_____   _____

_____   (____)_____

_____   _____

_____   (____)_____

_____   _____

_____   (____)_____

_____   _____

_____   (____)_____

_____   _____

_____   (____)_____

_____   _____

_____   (____)_____

_____   _____

_____   (____)_____

_____   _____

_____   (____)_____

Industry Influencers

Industry Influencers are those 10 percent in any niche industry who influence the other 90 percent. Know who these people are. Write to them. When you see that they have published or been written about, send them a copy of the article with your congratulations. Let them know that you are out there and admire their good work. These influencers can convince others to decide to use you, your product or your service.

Reading trade publications helps you to identify who influences whom in any niche market. When you are aware of who the influencers are, you can begin the process of networking through them to obtain all kinds of opportunities—jobs, product or service sales, more marketing opportunities (i.e., speaking engagements, co-sponsored events, etc.). Use the form in Figure 4.2 to help you build your base of influencers.

Making a Connection

You want someone who has a behavior that lends itself to networking (a proactive behavior) and someone who does have influence by position. Charlie Babbit, played by Tom Cruise in the movie *Rainman*, was a young man in pursuit of what he thought was his rightful share of his father's $3 million estate. To acquire his half, Charlie took his autistic brother Raymond out of the place where he was institutionalized. Charlie kept his brother as sort of a hostage to further negotiate his half of the estate.

After several days of caring for Raymond, Charlie began to realize the extent of the care that his brother needed. More importantly, Charlie realized how much he cared about his brother. When a hearing was held to

Figure 4.2 Industry Influencer Template

Name _____

Title _____

Company Name _____

Address _____

City_____ State _____ Zip Code _____

Phone _____ Fax _____

Seen In _____

Interests _____

_____

Values _____

His/Her Suppliers (Name, Address, Phone)_____

_____

_____

Who are his/her customers?_____

_____

Where has he/she worked previously?_____

_____

With which department does he/she interact regularly?

_____

Where does he/she live? Neighbors?_____

_____

_____

What associations does or did he/she belong to?

_____

What service clubs or community groups does he/she
participate in?_____

_____

People who can introduce you to the influencer

_____

Other Information _____

_____

determine Raymond's fate, Charlie declared his intent to accept responsibility for caring for Raymond for the rest of his life. However, the doctors in charge of the hearing, after listening to both Charlie and Raymond, indicated that they really didn't think that Charlie was capable of caring for Raymond. Charlie insisted that there was an important reason for keeping his brother with him, blurting out, "You see, we made a connection. We made a connection."

I can still see Charlie's face in my mind. His *connecting* with his brother brings about an awareness that he needs to feel needed. I'm sure that we have all felt certain types and degrees of connections with others. In the business world, there is also a need for quality connections. Many times connections become more important than the rationalization of why we choose to do things. Knowing our emotional depths can lead to a better understanding of the importance of building relationships with the people with whom we have a positive emotional connection. We can build new business opportunities for each other.

An associate I recently coached told me that there were a number of people with whom he would like to *connect*. He wanted to connect, for example, with an attorney to whom he had given a number of referrals during the past year. My associate had not asked the attorney for any return referrals and was thinking that now would be a good time to look for reciprocal referrals. My associate was feeling awkward about asking. I assured him that the focus of his discussions with the attorney should not be to ask for referrals today, but rather to exchange information. Instead, he should review what had been done in the past and then propose that he and the attorney look at the present and future opportunity to exchange.

I assured my associate that he had developed enough psychological leverage to ask for a *shared* exchange in the future. Taking this approach, the associate was able to feel comfortable about requesting a new type of relationship. Today my associate has developed a strong relationship with the attorney, and they regularly refer prospects to each other.

Stay Aware

I introduced you to AWARE in the Introduction. It is an acronym I created that stands for: Attention With Action Realizes Excellence. In creating awareness, the first step is to focus your attention on the important things—strategic actions that make the difference between a casual and a long-term relationship. In the process of creating a winning first impression, you must focus on what it is that you can build from to create an equal exchange. In an equal exchange, you're seeking relationships just as you would when selecting members of a team. This is your life support team. It takes just two people to start a team. Once you have your first teammate, you are ready to make a positive difference in one another's lives.

Being AWARE requires that you first focus your *Attention* on the sources you can benefit the most and who can return the support. Look for people whose actions reflect the kind of behavior you value.

For example, look for leaders who volunteer their time to worthy causes. Many of these people can be found working on committees for local organizations. They will be written about in your local and national newspapers and magazines. Check your local library to locate sources in targeted industry publications or *Who's Who* directories. Look for these sources at seminars and talks given at your local association meetings. Look first for local influencers. They're more accessible. They earned positions of influence through the support of others and as achievers are usually very open to continuing support. You can help them get more exposure (promotional support) first, through your actions, and later, through your growing base of contacts. Such people do enjoy exposure. That's why they're constantly being recognized by the local media.

One dynamic entrepreneur made it his business to help a number of influencers obtain more exposure. At a Chamber event, this entrepreneur was responsible for booking more than half the speakers! The speakers were all very successful leaders in their respective industries. The entrepreneur was able to act as the liaison between the speakers and attendees who wanted introductions. The entrepreneur ended up the recipient of many warm contacts and prospects. He also deepened his relationship with the influencers, making it that much easier to get in contact with them in the future. It didn't matter that he was a start-up entrepreneur with very little money in the bank. He was able to leverage the strength of the association with the strength of the speakers. Today this entrepreneur is able to go to almost any association he chooses and offer his assistance, which results in a similar opportunity.

Another strategy mentioned earlier for meeting influencers is to attend local association meetings. Sit in the front where it will be easier to meet the speakers. Take notes during their talk. Identify their emotional connection with their topic. Jot down a question or two on the back of one of your cards that addresses the interest of the speaker. If, for example, the speaker is talking about cost reduction, you might write, "Ms. Smith, what would you recommend that someone in my type of business do to cut costs?"

After the talk, quickly go up to the front of the room. Keep your question short, to the point and relevant.

Initially, respecting someone's time constraints is the best way to ensure a good first impression. First, however, thank the speaker. Say how much you appreciated his or her talk: "I really enjoyed your speech. You helped me see some areas where I could reduce costs that I had never thought about before."

Next, mention that you have written your question down and ask, "Would you mind if I contact you next week to ask a quick question that I have written on the back of my card?" This will give you a reason to call again. Most speakers will be very receptive to your request, although on occasion a speaker will say that he or she just can't find the time.

I have found that influencers often welcome talking to people with less authority. They may enjoy the ego boost they get from being the center of attention, or they may genuinely appreciate the opportunity to give something back. I regularly meet people who feel a genuine desire to share the knowledge they've gained. These people often become great referral sources, but perhaps more importantly, they become friends.

When you network effectively, you will create a casual but anticipated exchange. Your attitude makes the difference. You cannot exchange if you don't honestly believe that you deserve to be the recipient. However, by creating structure, you increase this opportunity. We facilitate the goals we are seeking to achieve through the creation of this structure.

Studies indicate that on average you will have to make five or more contacts (phone calls, mailings, etc.) to close a sale. The percentages are very similar when developing an ongoing exchange. When we meet someone, we need to understand that the first step is a *getting acquainted* stage. The last thing you want to do in a first stage is to become flustered by thinking too much about all the other things that will happen later. Therefore, take your time during this first stage to look for the other parties' interests, strengths and values. You may not even have the opportunity during a first encounter to exchange any of your information.

The best you can do during your first encounter is to create a connection or set up another encounter. The second encounter will be where your begin to lay the foundation for a continuous future exchange.

When you go to a networking event where you don't know anyone, it is wise to have a goal in mind—to meet people you would like to talk with further. It could be one person or it could be two or more people. Don't focus on trying to work the whole room; instead, focus on finding one or two people who are potential referral sources. Later, after you've become familiar with the organization through information you've acquired through referral sources, you will have a good overview of the best prospects. Now, you can strategize your approach. Remember, you only have one chance to make a good first impression.

One smart strategy for entering the inner circle of an organization would be to find out the name of the person in charge of membership. You might say, "I'm interested in attending one of your meetings. I am thinking about becoming a member of your organization. Would it be possible for me to be your guest at an upcoming event? Of course, I will pay my way, but I would like to meet others who could give me an idea of what they value most about the organization." Because many organizations today are undergoing dramatic changes, they are finding that attracting and keeping good members is getting more and more difficult. Therefore, most organizations will welcome having a proactive person like yourself inside where you can get involved and help the membership grow. If you stay proactive, you will have the opportunity to be introduced into the inner circle rather than wait years to connect to the top line of any organization. I found this technique to be especially successful when networking at large conventions.

Finding the Inner Circle

I was able to get involved with one of the organizations I find most beneficial for my business development—The National Speakers Association. Through one of its proactive members, Jeff Slutsky, author of several books, including *How To Get and Keep Clients*, I was able to enter the inner circle, meeting with accomplished authors and gaining wonderful insights into the world of writing and speaking.

You will find that association events unite people from all over the country and perhaps the entire world. Having someone introduce you can make all the difference. It is analogous to having a tour guide take you to places and show you the areas that most tourists never see. You become an insider, sharing the wealth of everyone's experiences and connections. These are the individuals you are looking for at the top 20 percent. You can be quickly introduced to them through key people in the organizations.

The focus is not on your attitude, but on the perception of the people you will be calling. An organization is interested in attracting qualified new members. You are displaying yourself as a very qualified member when you take the time to thoroughly investigate whether an organization would be beneficial to you and whether you would be beneficial as a member.

Many organizations are struggling to attract active new members. The decrease in their membership base offers you significant opportunity.

It's Not What You Do, but How You Do It

There will be times when you meet people and discover that the opportunity to develop a relationship just doesn't exist. The best thing you can do at this point is either introduce this person to another party or, if you don't know anyone else there, diplomatically excuse yourself by saying, "It was very nice meeting you. I look forward to talking to you again." Then move on.

Look for people whom you can help and who can help you. If this is not apparent in the first discussion, it may not be in future discussions. In looking for the best way to develop relationships, your goal is to look for ways to increase your chances of a long-term relationship. The best way to do this is to observe what matters to the influencer and ask open-ended questions. For example, one person may express interest in building quality relationships. Focus on what matters to others. These things will be conveyed as they discuss certain interests with you. When you pick up on someone's interest, let them know. You might say something like, "I share a similar interest in _____ (whatever you have noticed that you do share). I would love to talk more about this with you." Here you are acknowledging what the other person does, you are commending them and you are providing them with an opportunity for future discussion on common areas of interest.

In our over-communicated society, the paradox is that nothing is more important than communication. With communication skills that you've developed to your advantage, anything is possible. Without these skills, nothing is possible. No matter how talented and ambitious you may be, you need good communication skills.

As Al Ries and Jack Trout emphasize in their book, *Positioning: The Battle for Your Mind,* "In the communication jungle out there, the only hope to score big is to be selective. To concentrate on narrow targets. To practice segmentation. In a word, positioning."

Ries and Trout emphasize the importance of creating a position in someone else's mind. In this case, you are looking for the position of influence in the mind of your potential referral source. Ries and Trout further point out that, "What's called luck is usually an outgrowth of successful communication, saying the right things to the right persons at the right time."

There is no question that the science, and again I say *science*, of communication can be greatly improved when one is working off the interests of another. What you might consider difficult—creating conversations that are stimulating and motivating for others—is not what is really required. Instead, you are *appreciating* another person and adding to their interests by sharing your similar interests. The work is really being done by the other party. You simply take their lead and build from it.

You are providing the brick and mortar of the conversation. Together, you are building a foundation for future conversations. You build conversations based on the other parties' interests by matching their concerns with things that matter to you.

Let's say that someone you are talking with mentions being an avid sailor. Perhaps you know very little about sailing, but enjoy water sports. You mention your interests and listen appreciatively while the other person tells you about his sailing adventures.

The other person might say, "I like sailing because it's great to get away from work and relax." That's an opening for you to ask what other things the person does to relax. You might discover a similar interest that you both can share. One connection after another will lead you to other interests you share—*Points of Commonality* that will help to build rapport more quickly.

Seek out sources without regard to position. Once you build your basic network, other opportunities will come your way as a natural outgrowth of these primary relationships. As Ries and Trout point out, "It is possible to succeed in business or in life all by yourself. But it's not easy."

Business is, among other things, a social activity, and there will always be opportunities to communicate that lead to developing rapport and uncovering common interests. The good news is that for each of us there are people out there who are tailor-made for the kind of building we're looking to do—the building of future opportunities.

One of the best strategies that you can use for thinking big is to read publications that regularly research your target market. A number of general business and industry publications include lists on top people and businesses in targeted industries. I recommend the *Relational Directory* (312) 880-0089, which lists key individuals and corporations in city by city volumes. It's important to know who these people are because you'll never know when you might run into them in your initial stages of networking. Eventually, through the strategic process of building your network, you will be able to access these people through powerful introductions.

First Things First

You must know business trends, community and industry leaders and target market. Take the time to chart this information as follows:

Industry: Banking

Trends: Regulation issues, consolidations, lay-offs

Key Influencers:
>Charles A. Lewis, Merrill Lynch & Co.
>Edgar Jannotta, William Blair & Co.
>Scott P. George, Bankers Trust Company

Look for people and industries with whom these people are further connected. You would be surprised at how many clients I work with who have little knowledge of their competitors and even less knowledge of their prospect base. Look for contacts in articles published in business publications, such as *Entrepreneur, Home-Office Computing, Inc., Nation's Business, Success*, and your daily newspapers—many of which have success stories that run once a week. All of these publications are useful as you try to locate people who would be good referral sources.

One strategy that I have found to be particularly effective has been to call people who are featured in articles. These people often are available and always appreciate an acknowledgment of their accomplishments.

Additionally, there are many sources that you can acquire through lists. Alumni directories are a good place to start. Harris Publishing Company, (800) 877-6554, offers a number of alumni directories. Take time to reunite with past friends and fellow classmates. You will never know where they might be now or whom they might know unless you call.

Once you buy your lists, keep your eyes open for patterns. Who was in the paper and is now at the networking events you are attending? Is there an opportunity to be introduced to them? Tell these people that you will tell many other people about them (which you can and must do later). In turn, these people could be mentors who might provide you with assistance in growing your career and eventually provide you with referrals.

It is also important to know your top three competitors. I hesitate to use the word *competitor*, because the term has negative connotations. However, as a collaborative strategist who uses the MegaNetworking System, you should be aware so that you can differentiate yourself from others in your field. Know how you are unique. For instance, in my firm, we differentiate ourselves by offering value-added industry roundtables, such as special manufacturing roundtables focused on the special needs and interests of manufacturing companies.

By seeing others in your field as colleagues rather than competitors, you establish yourself as someone who is approachable. Identify the top five leaders in your area of specialty, and keep tabs on what they're doing. When asked about your competition, your knowledge of their work will actually increase your credibility with others.

Be genuinely interested in what your competitors do. Understand that in today's world there is a place for all those who are out there helping others build their dreams. Find out who would be the top ten most significant businesses in your target market.

Plan

People tend to forget that planning is not an exact science. Consumer and business needs change constantly. Your job, therefore, is to continually refocus on relationships and the process of development rather than the details of exactly what you've been given up to that point.

Your skill at developing relationships will improve over time. However, if you continue to think "I'm no good at sales or networking," you will limit your ability to improve. If you make this statement, alter it by saying, "Up until now I've not been good at sales or networking, but now I am quickly building the skills to be effective." In this way you give yourself permission to improve—which you will.

Ask good questions, and listen to understand. Work hard at actually hearing what others have to say. Listening—and remembering facts about other people—makes them feel important. You might say, "My experience is that _____ and _____ are the most important things happening in your industry. Do you agree?" Give your contact an opportunity to show how they think rather than just what you think. By asking, exploring, listening and then digesting the information, you can build to another level of understanding.

Steps to Building Your Base of Referral Sources

+ Look for the way people act, locating the most *proactive* sources first. Their positions of importance in their respective industries are of secondary importance.

+ Treat good sources just as you would good prospects. Consistently set aside time to meet and exchange resources.

+ Know the qualities of good referral sources. They are givers; they are involved in their local communities; they stay aware of your needs and interests; they are dependable; they are persistent throughout the peaks and valleys that are a natural part of the exchange. And, they share a common goal— going beyond the process of networking to a broader vision of work and success.

+ Locate the *influencers* in your industry. They are accessible if you first support their efforts.

+ Use industry influencers primarily as sources of information. They will lead you through the information jungle that stands between you and your opportunities.

+ Remember, the best strategy for building a great base of referral sources is to ask, ask and then ask some more. Keep asking to identify the best networkers. MegaNetworkers are out there—you will find them if you ask!

Step 3:
Creating Winning
First Impressions

"The networker must concentrate on the first part of the body that the listener sees: the face and especially, the eyes. Learn to use what I call an 'eye-alogue.' Prolonged empathetic eye contact, more penetrable than monologue and more disclosing than dialogue, eye-alogue establishes harmony immediately."

Dr. Gilda Carle
President, InterChange Communications

In the unlikely event that you have already located your entire base of referral sources through your existing contacts, it won't be necessary for you to read this chapter. However, if you're like most people, you will benefit from the strategies presented here.

Creating Rapport

You've just been introduced or introduce yourself to someone you've never met before. What do you say now? Start with general questions that identify your new contact's background: "George, what company are you with?—or—"George, what brings you to this meeting?" Notice that these questions are open-ended. They require more than a "yes" or "no" answer. Open-ended questions encourage others to *open up*. You want to encourage your new contacts to share as much information about themselves as possible. Each nugget of information will help you identify common interests—Points of Commonality that create rapport leverage. The more common interests you share, the more potential there is to grow the relationship. If your contact says, "I'm in the moving industry," see if they have connections to your area of interest. For example, if you're in the telecommunications industry, you might say, "That's very interesting. Do you work with anyone in the telecommunications field?" Chances are your new contact, depending on the number of years he or she has been in the industry, will have relationships with telecommunications people. However, it is best to hold off asking *who* is in their network. Asking too much too soon makes it seem as though you are only interested in yourself. If the contact offers information without too much probing, there is a strong possibility that this person will make a good referral source. Save a more in-depth conversation for the exchange. Your next step is to establish some points of credibility.

Points of Commonality and Credibility

Two very effective strategies for creating rapport start with building *Points of Commonality* and *Points of Credibility*.

Points of Commonality are developed from the interests and experiences you have developed throughout your life that when shared with contacts quickly build rapport. They are current or past interests that stretch as far back as childhood—like playing the violin, writing for the school newspaper or having gone to a particular camp. Think about these interests and experiences. List them in any order at first. Just brainstorm, writing down the first ideas that come to your mind. This list will create a good starting base that you can use to develop rapport with new contacts.

Example

1. Walking
2. Dancing
3. Swimming
4. Writing
5. Movies
6. Volunteer Work
7. Travel
8. Family
9. Music
10. Spiritual Activities

Your Turn

1.
2.
3.
4.
5.
6.
7.
8.
9.
10.

Now prioritize your list. Think for a couple of minutes before you begin to make sure that you have identified what interests matter most to you today. You may be surprised by your choices. There might be an interest that you thought wasn't as important, but when placed against your other interests, really is important. This activity will also help you plan your interpersonal relationships. You will have taken the time to articulate what you want in your exchanges with others.

Example

1. Spiritual
2. Family
3. Writing
4. Volunteer Work
5. Music
6. Movies
7. Travel
8. Walking
9. Dancing
10. Swimming

Your Turn

1. _____
2. _____
3. _____
4. _____
5. _____
6. _____
7. _____
8. _____
9. _____
10. _____

Continue to build rapport with Points of Credibility. Points of Credibility are developed from the strengths, accomplishments and values that are uniquely you. These characteristics create the foundation for every long-term relationship you will build. They can be shared in the early stages of a relationship, often in the initial exchange, resulting in an almost instant rapport and trust. This happens when there is *commonality*—where the contact shares similar strengths, accomplishments and values.

It is important to identify your strengths, accomplishments and values in advance. By identifying these points in advance you will be better able to take advantage of your unique characteristics to create better networking opportunities. Do this by writing them out now. Return to this page as often as you can to fine-tune this list of attributes. Over time you will begin to understand just how beneficial an awareness of your attributes can be.

Example

Your Top Three Strengths

1. Writing
2. Consulting
3. Speaking

Three Additional Strengths (as Identified by Friends, Family, Associates, etc.)

1. Caring and involved parent
2. Enthusiasm
3. A loyal, honest friend

Your Top Three Accomplishments

1. Writing two books
2. Acquiring a number of repeat consulting engagements with large companies
3. Facilitating a number of successful workshops

Three Additional Accomplishments (as identified by friends, family, associates, etc.)

1. <u>Speaking nationally</u>
2. <u>Nominated for entrepreneurial advocate awards</u>
3. <u>Featured in several national publications</u>

Your Top Three Values

1. <u>Integrity</u>
2. <u>Follow-through</u>
3. <u>Courage</u>

Your Turn

Your Top Three Strengths (Most Developed Skills)

1. _____
2. _____
3. _____

Three Additional Strengths (as Identified by Friends, Family, Associates, Etc.)

1. _____
2. _____
3. _____

Your Top Three Accomplishments

1. _____
2. _____
3. _____

Three Additional Accomplishments (as Identified by Friends, Family, Associates, Etc.)

1. _____
2. _____
3. _____

Your Top Three Values

1. _____
2. _____
3. _____

One of the individuals I coached did this exercise and discovered strengths that he didn't even know he had. Another associate found that she was not doing certain things that she thought she was doing. Arlene improved her skills by changing the way she dealt with people. Throughout her career, my associate had a tendency to "go with the flow"—allowing others to determine what was best for her. By looking over areas for improvement, Arlene found that she really did have a good idea of her strengths and that she did know what she wanted. So, when she had the opportunity, Arlene called one of the managing partners of our accounting firm and said to him, "I'm not the same woman I was a year ago, and I really think that I can do things differently now. I would like to be invited to certain sessions that other associates attend. Please think of me the next time that one of these opportunities comes to fruition for the firm." The managing partner was very impressed with Arlene's new found confidence! He saw her change into someone who was now interested in taking on new responsibilities and opportunities. She was now a motivated, proactive employee.

Developing Trust

Trust is essential to building an ongoing exchange of referrals. It takes time to develop trust, but that time can be dramatically shortened through a systematic approach where you create points of consensus through Points of Commonality and Points of Credibility. Rapport is a combination of timing, tone and content. (Keep in mind that communication is 50 percent body language, 40 percent tone of voice and 10 percent the actual words used.)

I have given you a number of strategies for building content, but without a genuine tone and effective timing, your content may sound contrived. Your tone reflects your attitude. This is where sincerity is a must. If you are not sincerely interested in what someone else has to say, you comments will most likely come across as insincere. There is no substitute for sincerity. The only way to develop it is to recognize that you need other people in your life, and they are just as important as you are. In fact, when building a MegaNetwork, you need other people much more than they need you.

Timing

Your timing is also important. If you take the time to listen, however, you should have less trouble with timing. When you focus your attention on listening twice as much as you talk, you will find timing is much less important. Your contacts will appreciate being listened to—an experience that they might not often have. As I mentioned in Chapter 4, it is important to listen actively—picking up on the things that matter most to your contacts. You can hear it in your contacts' tone; it will match their body language. Look at your contacts' eyes. You've probably seen people whose eyes *light up* when they are talking about something in which they have a strong interest. Ask questions that get to the heart of that person's interests. Be *other focused*. This means that if someone is telling you about the business they are engaged in, ask questions that build upon that person's interest.

For example, if someone tells you that they are involved in copier sales, you might say, "Tell me more about the type of people you come in contact with." Ask questions like a good journalist would ask in an interview, such as "What type of people usually buy your copiers?" "Where do you usually sell them?" "Why would someone buy your copier instead of another brand?"

By asking such questions, you are able to learn much more about how this person perceives his or her industry. You are looking for people who are proud of what they do and feel very comfortable describing their product and their market. When you actively listen, you are listening to *understand* what is important to another person. By *acknowledging* what they think is important, you share more intimately in their lives. You increase the quality of your relationships. You grow trust, which translates into building connections that refer business opportunities more easily and readily.

Communication Styles

Dr. Gilda Carle, a specialist in communications, suggests using what she calls, *Eye-alogue, Dialogue, Monologue.* As Carle points out, "Most people usually demonstrate a predisposition for one of three styles of communicating—visual, auditory or kinesthetic (feeling)." Carle recommends that we become aware of the style of the people with whom we are talking. So, if you know people who often use words like "I see," you would mirror their vocabulary by saying things like, "I see your point." These people are more visually oriented.

For those who are auditory communicators, you might say, "I hear what you're saying." Finally, for those with more of a kinesthetic style of communication, you might say, "I understand how you feel."

Other people don't consciously recognize when you adapt to their communication style; your vocabulary adjustments trigger strong connections with their sub-conscious. This is another good reason to allow the other party to talk more. You will pick up hints from the other person's vocabulary and adapt your conversation to their style, increasing the chances of building rapport.

Avoid people who are argumentative. You will see this as a recurring pattern in their behavior if you choose to continually network with them.

Exchanging

To lead from your strengths in a discussion, talk about some of the things that you do. More likely than not, you will be asked about them. Now you have the opportunity to share those things that you're good at and that you're interested in doing.

For example, when someone asks me what I enjoy doing, I usually respond, "Writing, speaking, negotiating, collaborating." My focus in an initial meeting is to listen 80 percent of the time, and talk 20 percent of the time. In the initial exchange, I seek a way to provide at least three of the elements of the Five-Part Assist.

For example, if you find that someone is in a particular industry and you've heard of a trade show coming up in that industry, mention it. Now you have a value-added exchange. That person will remember your consideration and interest and will probably offer something in return.

I recommend against providing referrals in an initial exchange because you have not yet had the opportunity to really develop a relationship with this person. The referral would involve putting yourself more or less on the line, and it would therefore be best that you keep your initial exchange to information, promotion, emotional support and leads.

Top Strategies for Creating Winning Impressions

The top strategies for building a winning impression are:

- *Polish your image.* Create a positive image that will attract people through consistent caring behavior.

- *Stay other-focused.* Continue to focus on the needs, wants and problems of others. Remember that this is still an exchange, and you will be looking for responsive action on the part of those you do business with. Is this person a good listener? Does he or she care about what you have to offer? Does he or she respect who you are?

- *Ask, explore, listen and digest.* First, listen for understanding. When you listen for understanding, you are listening for more than information. You are making sure that you see what is important in the information that has been given to you. One effective strategy is to paraphrase what was said to make sure that you have understood thoroughly and to show you've been listening.

- *Learn to prioritize.* Listen for another person to indicate needs and interests. Ultimately you are looking for gaps in someone's existing network where you could provide a service that is not currently available or offer a service that is superior to something that is being provided. Here, a knowledge of your competitors is very important, as well as a knowledge of your uniqueness. Create a winning impression during your first encounter.

- *Help your contacts picture in their minds the benefits that others could receive by using your product or service.* Get them excited about these benefits so that they adopt your enthusiasm and, in turn, pass it on to prospects.

- *Ask both open-ended and close-ended questions to build agreement that what you have to offer is indeed desirable.* Your contacts can be very instrumental in providing you with feedback as to the interest there might be in purchasing the services or products that you have to offer.

- *Carefully observe body language.* You need to build agreement in a way that is most appealing. For example, lean closer, nod, smile, etc.

- *Become a specialist.* Time and time again experts in sales agree that generalists end up losing ground to specialists. Become a specialist and then get the word out about your specialty. When you specialize in a particular industry or develop a particular skill, you will have a better opportunity to penetrate a market more quickly, because there will be fewer people in your market who have the same skills and expertise.

- *Know your "Giveability Quotient."* In networking, you need to promote yourself. But the focus is initially on the other party. Your success will be in direct proportion to your perceived ability to give. Many, many people fear that they don't have a high giveability quotient. Realize that this is not an uncommon fear. Remember that in all the relationships that you have had thus far—although they have not been necessarily for business—you have been exchanging and offering one thing in return for another. When you were a student, you offered your work for a grade. With your parents, you offered caring and participation in your family in exchange for a roof over your head and food to eat. Those of you who have married offer numerous means of assistance in exchange for participating in a family environment. Everyone has been involved in a series of exchanges. When networking, be aware of what you are giving and what is expected of you. The Five-Part Assist is an excellent reminder of how much more you have to give than you usually realize.

- *Stay aware.* Remember, Attention With Action Realizes Excellence. It's not what you *say* you're going to do, it's what you *do* that matters. Watch what people do, not what they say. The only real marketing awareness we have is the activity, the behavior of our contacts. Relationships do take time, but through all the processes of setting up a structure for maximum exchange potential of referrals, you will learn quickly who is really giving and who is not. You will create a record of this in your Referral Source Meeting Summary. (See Appendix IV.)

- *Present yourself as the solution to others' problems.* People are constantly looking for solutions and improvements to their situations. In business, you can offer so much more if you approach others as the solution to current problems and future problems.

- *Build appreciation into your meetings with others.* When you appreciate others, as mentioned before, challenge yourself to be specific. For example, if someone has taken the time to purchase new clothes or something that is unique or special about them, comment about it. It will make the other person feel better, and when people feel better about themselves, they are more open to sharing. A trick is to look for things that people say with an added emotional emphasis. For example, if someone says, "Gee, I started a new business!" you might respond: "I'm so excited for you. Congratulations."

From there, work off of your contact's enthusiasm. It will connect you to other conversational exchanges that will grow over time.

◆ *Be a good listener and a good encourager.*   The greatest gift you can give to others is to lend them your ears.

Networking Etiquette

There are certain rules of etiquette that will help you be a more effective networker. They include remembering to:

◆ Tell people you meet that you will follow up in the next day or two, and then make sure that you do follow up. Your actions will show that you are a professional.

◆ Maintain eye contact. There is nothing more annoying than people who don't look at you when they talk to you.

◆ Keep smiling. Smiling shows people that you are open and eager to listen to them. More than anything you say or do, a genuine smile is your most powerful networking tool.

◆ Locate people who are standing alone. You know how you feel when you are alone. Helping someone else feel welcome by acting as a host even if you are a guest will also help you feel more at ease.

◆ Give first, before you ask for anything. Be the gracious host, looking first to make others comfortable and only then addressing your own needs.

◆ If you choose to move to another contact at a networking event, kindly excuse yourself. Don't spend all your time with one contact while continuously gazing around the room for a "better" opportunity.

Find ways to interrupt without stopping the flow of conversation when there is a group that has already gathered. A very good technique is to stand at the side and listen enthusiastically with expressive body and facial language.

First Impressions and the Fear of Rejection

Overwhelmingly, people fear rejection. It is not the rejection itself, but the actual fear of it, as Jack Lemmon once said, that causes us to avoid meeting new people. I prefer to think of all the opportunities that I'm missing when I don't connect, when I don't reach out. I realized that I would not have the benefit of the knowledge and the support of others if I didn't risk. Through risking, even though I would experience a certain amount of rejection, I did have faith that others would be more like me—wanting and appreciating others who would listen to them and support their efforts. Truly, that is what I've found.

Visualization

When you put things in perspective, you gain from each experience. Think of all the ideas and opportunities that you'll be missing if you fear encountering others. One technique that I find useful in overcoming rejection is visualization. Visualization gives you a sense of purpose. Remember as a child, you might have been accused of doing something wrong. You would respond to your accusers, "But I didn't *mean* to do it."

Now, you have a different choice—to do things on purpose. When you visualize, visualize a new scene—a scene with you accomplishing things.

If you have trouble visualizing, try talking yourself through a visualization or writing it out. You might also pick up *Creative Visualization* by Shakti Gawain, an excellent book for guiding you through the process. Through visualization you will create a state of positive expectation.

I started the process of visualization and meditation about three years ago. It took a good two years for me to feel extremely comfortable with the process and to use it in a way that empowered me on an ongoing basis. Today visualization is such a part of my life and such a useful tool that I am able to avoid spiraling downward into a state of depression by recognizing a situation that might set into course a series of other problems. Again, it's the little things that always make the difference. You don't want to have any actions on your part used against you. Instead, you want to continually look at the opportunities life presents you. Visualization helps you take your expectations and put them into a favorable light so that you will be able to actualize them.

All thoughts are the germs of real things that can manifest in positive ways in your life. Or they can manifest themselves in very negative ways. It is always your choice.

Rejection

Rejection is a temporary situation. The thought by the rejector is not ours. We did not create it. When we reach outside of ourselves for approval, we are guaranteed to find a certain amount of rejection. This is very natural. Sometimes it is because other people don't understand us, and other times it is for reasons that are even silly— you remind them of someone else with whom they once had a bad experience. When you are confident about yourself you won't judge yourself, and if others judge you, it will not concern you.

Carol Hyatt and Linda Gottlieb provide a comprehensive look at failure and our attitudes toward it in their book, *When Smart People Fail.* Addressing the similarities between success and failure, the authors provide a description of a well-known actress—an Academy Award nominee—who had become unemployed when the television series that came from a movie for which she had been nominated was canceled. While her younger, unknown co-stars quickly lined up engagements, she was not as successful. As the other co-stars were looking forward to their new and exciting opportunities, all this actress had to look forward to was the unemployment line. However, the actress was prepared to go back to that line and begin again. Her attitude of acceptance rather than defeat was based upon her knowledge that these setbacks happen again and again. In her broader perspective, she was able to put the setback into perspective.

Hyatt and Gottlieb point out that success and failure are cyclical, reappearing throughout one's lifetime. When risks are taken, setbacks are part of the process. In fact, they are very natural. The authors point out that neither success nor failure should be taken too seriously.

Seek to gain a sense of peace and satisfaction from within. Avoid letting outside situations take you on a downward emotional spiral that turns into unhealthy depression. I mentioned before that a certain amount of dissatisfaction can actually be good. You can use those feelings as catalysts to motivate you to accomplish your goals. However, if you let your feelings of unrest turn into feelings of helplessness, you may require professional help.

Reducing Stress and Anxiety

Ellen McGrath, a specialist in stress and anxiety reduction recommends the following five action strategies:

1. Write or draw your feelings.
2. Take a walk.

3. Develop creativity.
4. Build and maintain connections at work and home.
5. Help others.

McGrath emphasizes that the most important thing you can do is to have action strategies prepared ahead of time. By developing two or three strategies, you can quickly move from an unproductive emotional state to a more positive productive state. Your actions will come first; the healthier emotions they create will develop later.

One action step might be to develop a private statement about yourself that clearly describes who you are. For example, "I am a kind, honest person who sincerely wants to succeed and help others whenever possible." When you find someone who threatens that statement, go back to it. If you have taken the time to be honest with yourself, you will find that your statement holds emotional credibility. As a result, a statement from the outside won't hold the same strength. When you own your own thoughts, you will no longer be the slave of other people's thoughts

Perception

I know a consultant who was expanding his career through public speaking. He got the word out to his network that he wanted to start speaking, and before long he received a call from a group asking to retain him as a speaker at an upcoming meeting. The consultant prepared diligently, even taking seminars on how to prepare a professional speech. On the day of the speech, the speaker was prepared and gave an informational talk with a sound base of motivational rhetoric. When the speaker finished, he was asked a number of questions. As he stepped down from the stage, he was involved in talking with people who paid him compliments for the next 45 minutes. The speaker was very pleased. Of course, he was open for improvement, but he had accomplished setting into motion a new marketing strategy to bring in more clients. He thought everything was wonderful. Until later.

My friend received a call from the Program Committee chairperson who told him that she wanted to review the speech with him. She said that the speech hadn't been what she had hoped to receive. She appreciated his efforts, but she would have liked him to have offered more *sophisticated* strategies.

The rejection bothered my friend tremendously. Did this mean that he should give up his speaking career? My friend decided to take the chairperson's criticism constructively, breaking apart her opinion from fact. The facts were the strategies that he could use to improve next time.

My friend knew that there would be a next time if he was willing to continue risking. He created a comprehensive questionnaire that addressed questions, such as, "What level of knowledge does the audience currently have on this subject?" and "What are the top three or four questions they might have on this subject?" My friend learned that rejection could be used as a tool for continuous improvement rather than as a permanent roadblock to success.

Rejection can be turned into constructive feedback, if broken down, separating fact from opinion. This proactive way to address rejection can ultimately improve future performance and help you reduce the emotional strain of rejection. Flat, cold rejection based on age, race or gender, should be placed in a totally different category. In the initial stages of creating your primary network, avoid people who exhibit this type of prejudice.

The entrepreneur's acceptance of rejection can be even higher, because they are constantly faced with having to sell a new or additional service or product. It is particularly important for entrepreneurs and sales reps to realize that rejection must not be internalized. Entrepreneurs have to produce, deliver and continue to service the client until they are no longer needed. If you are an entrepreneur, you will find yourself having a constant commitment to a wide variety of customer responsibilities.

One of the things that I've used effectively, is to internalize things that motivate me rather than demotivate me. In turn, I seek to say things to people that will empower or motivate them rather than demotivate them. In our guilt-ridden society, no one wants to admit responsibility. There's always the tendency to find someone else to blame.

Don't take advantage of other people, and don't let other people take advantage of you. Be clear about what you know is right for you and what you stand for. When you are grounded in your values, rejection will have a minimal impact on your attitude.

Risk Taking and First-Time Networking

When you make an initial contact with someone, you may feel awkward, incompetent or just plain SCARED! Expect to feel some fear, it's very natural. Even top networkers sometimes experience the fear of meeting new people. But ask yourself what you want. When you meet people who might help you locate prospects or are prospects themselves, make it worthwhile. One successful networker offers these suggestions:

> When I first started networking, I was completely overwhelmed. I finally understood that it is part of the natural process of meeting new people. I could set a reasonable goal of talking to two new contacts and working up from that. Before you run, you have to crawl, then walk.

If you feel awkward, it is normal. Just don't set yourself up for failure. Your initial goal should be to exchange *information*. If you focus only on your discomfort, you

Figure 5.1 Thinking Better! Five Steps to Overcoming Rejection

Fortunately, there are *preventive* measures that you can take to stop the severe results of repeated rejection. Use this exercise over the next 21 days. (Remember it takes at least three weeks to form a good or bad habit.) Any time you experience what you perceive as rejection (your perception is your reality), sit down in a quiet place as soon as possible, and answer these five questions

1. Name of person who rejected you _____

2. Position of person _____

3. What did that person say to you? (Try to remember it word for word.) _____
_____
_____
_____

4. What would you rather have heard? (Here, be as positive as possible. Use words that motivate *you*.)
_____
_____
_____

5. What logical steps could you take to change this situation?_____
_____
_____

Example

1. Name of person who rejected you Mr. Andrew Smith

2. Position of person Head of Training for Baker McNeil—law firm

3. What did that person say to you? (Try to remember it word for word.) "Send me something, and I'll look at it at *my* leisure."

Figure 5.1 Thinking Better! Five Steps to Overcoming Rejection (Continued)

4. What would you rather have heard? (Here, be as positive as possible. Use words that motivate *you*.)

   <u>"I'd be happy to have a meeting with you. Your company sounds very exciting—just what we've been looking for!"</u>

5. What logical steps could you take to change this situation?

   a. Work through my network of contacts who might either know Mr. Smith or know someone who knows him and can give me some insight into his personality. For example, knowing he is this way with most people would make me feel better. Here I can also find out what it takes to get him in a way that would appear more positive to me.

   b. Send my sales literature with a letter thanking him for his interest—stay positive. Show in the letter all the benefits of my service—but write the letter with Mr. Smith's personality in mind.

   c. Call Mr. Smith again, and if I get what I perceive as rejection again, try saying, "Mr. Smith, can you help me? I believe my service could be useful to your firm. Yet, the only way to find that out would be to meet for ten minutes or less. I don't want to waste your time, therefore, would next Wednesday or Thursday be convenient for you?

   d. If you get an appointment, give yourself a small reward.

   Follow up: <u>Met with Mr. Smith. Found out we could offer his employees a time management program. Have been working with them now for three months. They are very pleased. I am now looking at presenting a team building training program for their senior partners.</u>

will build a big block of self-consciousness. Instead, focus on other people. In time, a number of these contacts will turn into your supporters and provide a solid network base.

Use your fear positively. Direct it into positive energy and actions. Fear directed negatively keeps us stuck. Face your fear. When someone says, "I'm not interested," ask, "Why?" This information will help you gain a better understanding as to what to do differently the *next time*. Understand also that there will always be people who will think either *less* or *more* of you than you think they should. Being prepared for some amount of rejection will not hinder your chances of building a very large, strong network. There are hundreds of people out there who will support you. Keep an open attitude, and you will find them. Truly, it's easier than you think.

The Dormant Connection

What connections do others have currently that you could use? The way to find these dormant connections is to ask questions. One person, even if he or she has a nominal number of contacts, could be a treasure to you or others you know. By mining other connections, you will be able to begin matching one person's connections to another person's interests. Take off the labels and titles of people. Be aware that we all tend to put labels on others and that the most important thing we can do in mastering the MegaNetworking matrix is to remove the labels from everyone and focus, instead, on personalities.

Ask yourself questions to lead you to new referral sources. For example, who do you know in the computer industry? In turn who do they know? Ask everyone. It's amazing how even the best salespeople forget to ask these questions.

There is a Chinese proverb that reads, "Tell me, and I'll forget. Show me, and I might remember. Involve me, and I'll understand." By involving others in your world, they will understand you. In understanding you, those who are open to an exchange will be the 20 percent who provide you with 80 percent of your results. Here, the Pareto Principle can work to your advantage in leveraging those hand-picked individuals who can help you achieve your MegaNetwork.

 ## Steps to Creating Winning First Impressions

- It's up to us to tell ourselves that we matter. From there, we will unleash great personal power. Without a commitment to Continuous Personal Development (CPD) on a daily basis, we will not grow.

- If you are not growing, you are losing ground. Be aware that you are not in this alone. There are many others out there looking for an alliance.

- An ongoing commitment to CPD will build a mountain of opportunities for you tomorrow. But the ultimate win is to locate other quality sources to co-create a stream of endless referrals.

- Use Points of Commonality to build an awareness of common interests with your contacts.

- Use Points of Credibility to accelerate the process of establishing rapport and move instead toward the more advanced exchange.

- Rapport takes us to the language of the individual. Good listening and a focus on understanding and trust will build a tailored bridge of communication between you and each person you meet.

Step 4:
Mastering the
Exchange

MegaNetworkers are self-starters who take responsibility for creating their own opportunities. Through a
process of *exchanges*, MegaNetworkers build an environment of trust and respect—two key elements conducive
to generating good business opportunities.

The exchange is the core of successful networking. It
starts as a spontaneous encounter at an event or during
a phone conference that resulted from a referral. Eventually, however, you must set up a more formal, structured
exchange—either a phone appointment or a one-on-one
meeting.

During this preplanned exchange, many things can
happen. Your goal is to maximize the outcome by co-
creating as many connections as possible for each other.
To achieve this goal, your focus needs to be on quality
rather than quantity. The following tips offer an overview of this process:

- *Find the we between the you and the me.* As you focus on co-creating opportunities for one another, ask, "What can we do for each other?" rather than, "What can you do for me?"

- *Brainstorm.* Your exchange requires brainstorming, the same type of activity that many authors use to create new written material. The Referral Source Meeting Summary (see page 105) provides the foundation for brainstorming during the exchange.

- *Withhold judgment.* Don't assume anything during the brainstorming phase of the exchange. Relax and enjoy this time to build rapport between you and your referral source. Judging sets up negative expectations. By withholding judgment, you will be able to create the highest quality connections.

- *Ask "Who do you know?" and "Do you know?"* There is a difference. Ask "who do you know?" when you're looking for people your referral source would know within any given industry. Ask "do you know?" when you have become familiar with the particular name of a prospect that you would like to contact, and you are asking your referral source for an introduction.

- *Stay focused on the Referral Source Meeting Summary.* The Summary (see page 105) is a useful tool to keep you focused on an equal exchange. If you fail to continually use this worksheet, you will find yourself returning to the vague world of passing information, leads and referrals in an ad hoc, disorganized fashion.

- *Always begin with emotional, promotional and information support before you talk about leads and referrals.* Build rapport by using the first three parts of the Five-Part Assist, and you will find yourself the recipient of many more leads and referrals.

- *Listen carefully to your referral source and respond with similar wording.* When you develop a similar language and usage of words, you accelerate the process of generating leads and referrals. This mirroring also helps develop consensus and understanding, which will further lead your referral source to creating connections for you.

- *Ask the same question twice.* You don't always have to ask the same question in the same way. However, by asking a question again, you may discover an answer that is much deeper and more genuine than if you had just asked a question once—especially those questions that you have regarding a potential prospect. Get to know as much as you can about the people to whom you are referred.

- *Always schedule follow-up meetings.* Never leave your referral source without setting up another meeting. Even if you cannot meet in person, set up a phone meeting. Phone meetings are very effective; as long as you remember to keep those appointments.

Master the Exchange

Your agreement to exchange creates trust, which allows you to *challenge* yourself and your source to dig deeper into your respective bases to unearth the best referrals

It usually takes three meetings before you master the exchange. At that point you will become familiar with the unique language patterns of your source. You will also utilize more effectively the Five-Part Assist presented in Chapter 2. As you will recall, the Five-Part Assist includes: emotional, promotional and information support, leads and referrals. You will find that during the first and second meetings you are still developing a common language that both of you will use to understand one another's interest and presentation styles. There are many people-reading tools that can assist with these first meetings, such as Meyers Briggs, the Predictive Index, Performax products, etc. Take a look to see which of these tools might assist you in the process of understanding and developing relationships faster.

The most important objective of the exchange is to communicate your needs and then educate your referral source to be the best salesperson for you. The time you spend educating is both necessary and valuable.

The next section will guide you step-by-step through the phases of the referral source meeting, so that you can develop similar meetings and achieve the results that come from a more structured setting.

Once you develop the skill to run a meeting effectively, you will no longer need this structure. However, just as with the development of any skill, it is helpful to have a little more structure in the beginning, so that you will be able to move from the beginning to the end of the process and understand all the phases in between.

The Referral Source Meeting

Exchange Current Information

During the initial meeting, you may find yourself feeling uncomfortable passing someone a copy of the Referral Source Meeting Summary. I sometimes use the form at an initial meeting; at other times I wait until a second or third meeting. I either take the form with me and fill it in myself, or fill it in *after* the meeting. However you use the form, it is important to move from one step to the next through the process of exchanging questions.

During Step One, offer your source any recent information you have gathered: current events, people you've come

Figure 6.1   Referral Source Meeting Summary

Lead/Referral (circle)   **Source** (list)

Name/Title_____

Company Name_____

Address_____

City/State/Zip_____

Telephone_____

Meeting Information

Today's date/time_____

Last meeting date/time_____

Next meeting date/time_____

Section I - Referral Log of Names

Name	Telephone	Address	Rank
_____	_____	_____	_____
_____	_____	_____	_____
_____	_____	_____	_____
_____	_____	_____	_____
_____	_____	_____	_____

Section II - Project Collaborations

_____

_____

_____

_____

_____

Section III - To Do (prioritize)

1._____

2._____

3._____

4._____

5._____

Section IV - (a) Who do you know? or (b) Do you know?

_____

_____

_____

_____

_____

in contact with, places you've visited or organizational meetings you have attended. All of these are useful topics for initial discussion.

By focusing your attention on the most recent connections of your source and yourself, you will find that you will more easily build other connections to additional contacts. The mind processes the most familiar information first, and with that information, there is the strongest depth of awareness.

Focus Your Attention on Your Referral Source's Current Base of Contacts, Prospects and Other Referral Sources

Shift from the most immediate relationships that you and your referral source have formed since your last meeting to the long-term potential that you can create over time. This step will take longer; most people don't carry their network base around in their head! Your sources will have to think about whom they know and how well they know them, as well as the level of influence that they have with those people.

Throughout the process, and when working on the Referral Source Meeting Summary, you need to use the section called *Rank* (See Referral Source Summary). *Rank* is the degree of influence that your referral source currently has with a particular connection. Ask your sources to estimate the level of influence they have with referred contacts and prospects on a scale from one to five, with one being a low degree of influence with another, and five being a very high degree of influence. Again, this ranking gives you a gauge to help assess how to prioritize whom you will contact first and what the likelihood is of developing a stronger relationship with that referred individual.

Create Action Steps

Talk about what each of you will do between now and the next time you meet. When you have completed brainstorming for contacts, prospects and other referral sources, start to ask yourselves what you can do individually between this meeting and the next to provide each other with emotional information and promotional support. For instance, if you are planning to attend a particular event or meeting, ask what you can do for the other party. What would the other party like to hear you say to others to promote the source's business? Ask for something in return. The Meeting Summary encourages an equal exchange. Use it as often as possible.

One opportunity that was created as a result of this step included a referral source that I was working with who had mentioned that she had a strong relationship with the Chicago Society of Association Executives organization (CSAE). This particular organization has a base comprised of association executives. I was very interested in making a presentation to them, so that I could get maximum exposure to a variety of other organizations.

My source, Jane Ranshaw, an excellent marketing consultant in Chicago, had given me the name of the program director and I had no trouble getting in to create the opportunity to present to the group. However, we might never have unearthed that opportunity if we hadn't asked the right questions of one another. So it is very important to move to this step and ask these questions, taking time for each source to reflect and exchange.

You will find that there will be many connections that you did not recognize until you move through this step. From one connection to the next, you will see that more and more opportunities arise.

During one exchange that occurred while brainstorming with a referral source, I provided my source with tips on being aware of opportunities to create connections wherever you go. In turn, the source had taken one specific tip and developed it. When she took her dog to the veterinarian, my source noticed that the building was becoming run-down. My source, a manager at a construction company, asked her vet if there was a possibility that he might be interested in remodeling his office. He said, "Thank you for bringing that up. In fact, several other veterinarians and I are looking to open a clinic." Being in the construction business, my source was very excited to have discovered this opportunity and mentioned that she would not have thought to attempt any connections until I had provided her with this strategy.

As a result of locating a new opportunity, my source needed an architect with experience in building clinics. At that point, I remembered an architect I had not been in touch with for at least a year. In fact, this architect's husband is a veterinarian, and she had been involved in designing his clinic. I recommended her to my source. This referral later resulted in a reunion between myself and the architect.

During some meetings I take my base or partial base of contacts with me. I find that there are always connections I don't make on my own that my sources see as beneficial. Consider taking your contact list with you, and encourage your sources to do the same. You will dramatically accelerate the exchange.

Summarize What You Have Given One Another, and Set the Next Meeting Date

This step is crucial to staying connected and will lead you to build opportunities from one contact to the next, one prospect to the next, one referral source to the next and one meeting to the next. It is often difficult to coordinate follow-up meetings, but taking the time to do so the first time and then the second makes it much easier the third, fourth and fifth times. Remember, always take the initiative. Don't wait for your source to contact you.

Eventually you will find that many of these meetings can be set up prior to your workday, after your workday and during lunch hours. I've even found that some of my conversations are held on Sunday evenings. Not everyone is interested in networking on the weekends and yet, once you become very good at the process, the meetings can be as short as ten minutes and yet be very effective.

There are many benefits to creating the exchange, but none as great as the continuous connection with quality referral sources. Take the time to find the best sources up front, and you will benefit for years and years to come.

The operative word here is the *exchange*. Watch out for what I call "Front End Loading." This is where you end up giving your referral source many contacts and connections and end up with very few in return. The purpose of the Referral Source Meeting Summary is to prevent that from happening. Many people are reluctant to ask for any type of assistance. The worksheet will provide that assistance.

It all comes down to processing information more effectively. The Meeting Summary creates connections as no verbal form of communication can. It is interesting to note that networking has been predominantly a verbal activity. And yet, by combining it with a visual tool like the Summary and placing structure behind it through continuous meetings, its power is tripled.

The Language of the Exchange

Whether you set up a referral source meeting or find yourself face-to-face with someone who can provide you with some type of connection, you are constantly picking and choosing words that will facilitate the exchange. One of the best phrases I have heard comes from a colleague, Susan Fignar, who says, "I would really appreciate the *opportunity* to assist you or anyone else you might know who would be able to benefit from the services my company offers." Susan, an image consultant, speaks with a calm tone mixed with warm enthusiasm. Her intent is to help others. It is this benefits-based focus that enables Susan to acquire a large group of new prospects and clients in a very short time.

When you start with the language of benefits, you begin to understand the focus of the exchange in a way that many networkers are unable to develop, even after years of networking. Note that there is a big difference between what you do and how you can help others.

A benefits-focus requires the following:

+ a focus on identifying the needs of others prior to identifying what you need;

+ an understanding of the specific needs that your referral source or contact has; and

+ a sincere effort to provide your sources with the connections they seek.

These points add up to listening, gaining an under-standing and being benefits-focused with your language. For example, if you are an attorney who specializes in new business start-ups and corporate law, you would say, "Hi, I'm John Smith from Smith and Tower. I special-ize in corporate law and help others with incorporating; creating partnership agreements and forming limited liability companies.

When you focus on benefits to others, you match what you can do with the needs they have or might have in the near future. On the other hand, if your focus is on what you do, and there has been no need identified or addressed, there is no connection made between a need and possible assistance.

Remember that at the heart of your words are your values. You must create a relationship based on shared values with your sources. Your values serve as the building blocks for future exchanges.

How the Exchange Helps Us See Our Blind Spots

We all have blind spots in our awareness. Because one large opportunity consists of many connected, smaller opportunities, it is very important to have others alert us to possibilities we may miss. Their added eyes and ears can continuously recognize new business and career opportunities.

When I finally let go of the challenge of trying to be *out there* all of the time, I was surprised by the power of my network. My network has helped me develop a sense of what I want—I ask for referrals for speaking engagements. This strategy offers me the biggest and best return on my networking efforts. As a speaker, I am more or less *endorsed* as a credible expert on my topic. People who come to see me buy into what I am saying. I usually end up with several potential referral sources, several prospects and clients. By asking only for referrals for speaking engagements, the effort I ask of my sources is easy, clear and achievable.

We all share the exact same numbers of hours in a day. Not one of us can duplicate ourselves. That's why getting others to exchange with us should be our ultimate goal.

To build quality exchanges:

+ Keep your request simple.
+ Work off of current relationships.
+ Educate your referral sources on *how* you sell.
+ Never leave a meeting without setting up another one.

- ◆ Focus first on the kind of people you would like to work with and the kind of work you want to do.

Realize that successful networking is a planned result, just as a bridge or a building is a planned result. Without deliberate networking plans, there will be no prosperous results on a consistent and permanent basis.

The Magical MegaNetworking Metamorphosis

Too many networkers think of referrals as one-way streets. They take referrals, but never give anything back to their sources, which then dry up. The MegaNetworker not only returns leads and referrals, but is proactive in doing so. The result is a continuous cycle of referrals. Ultimately, the process of building effective exchanges is tied in closely to mastering the Five-Part Assist. As mentioned earlier, the Five-Part Assist is crucial to building a MegaNetwork. Integrate the five parts into the exchange as follows:

Emotional Support. When you exchange emotional support, you are showing the other person that you care about them. Through your actions, you offer a connection that is stronger than any other type of connection you can create. When you actively *appreciate* others, you do so by using language and behavior that exemplify the caring individual.

A number of the people whom I have coached have utilized some of the techniques for appreciating others emotionally. One woman invited an employee who worked for her out to lunch and told this person how much she appreciated her work. This was not mandatory. There was no required job review session. Yet, this woman recognized how important it would be to appreciate her employee. A company's employees are its most valuable assets, although they often tend to be taken for granted. Providing emotional support to this group is extremely valuable, because they are *inside* as well as *outside* influencers for the company.

When we go out of our way at a time when praise is not expected, it is instead received as a surprise, which has a much stronger emotional impact. The dedication to building a positive emotional relationship with another party—employee, contact, referral source—creates an environment of trust. We build bridges of trust that enable us to weather any problems that might arise in the future through mis-communication or even the trouble associated with finding the time to keep in touch with contacts and referral sources.

Many opportunities for exchanges will grow from your use of appreciation.

Promotional Support. Promotional support creates a base of people who are continuous public relations agents for you. When you are not able to attend meetings or meet everyone you'd like to, your sources will be out there representing you and promoting you. The building of promotional support has tremendous power, especially if one is networking in a particular industry niche.

It doesn't take long for good news to spread. Perhaps this is because good news is not necessarily a common form of communication. For whatever reason, having promoters out there—people who will continuously be proactive in mentioning your name and the type of expertise that you have in your chosen field—has tremendous potential for creating better and better career and business opportunities for you.

When Janet Hansen was exhibiting at a trade show, she discovered the power of promotional support. Publisher of *The Business Woman's Advantage,* a unique newsletter for women entrepreneurs in Illinois, Janet was approached by many people who said they had heard good things about the publication. Seeing Janet made it a perfect opportunity for them to purchase subscriptions. The reputation of the newsletter combined with the work of Janet's network resulted in strong sales results.

Take the time to educate others as to the words they could use to promote you. Be very clear about what you would want others to say about you. If, for example, you are interested in building a new opportunity for yourself, consider mentioning this to your network and asking them to mention it to others.

You can use all the promotional support that you can get. Your network can proactively promote you in a way that you cannot promote yourself. This *third-party endorsement* is much more powerful than anything that you can initiate on your own. Everyone has their own network, and within these networks they can promote you. Your referral sources have built a bridge of credibility with those in their network and can create a bridge for you through their endorsements.

Information Support. Information support is like having a team of information specialists constantly acquiring and transmitting data back to you. It's like having a market research firm at your disposal. It's exciting to be surrounded by a network that is continually observant and aware of the types of information you would like to receive. You can be sent everything from articles concerning particular areas of interests, to telephone calls regarding shows that you should watch, to information about events that your network regards as important for you to attend.

Information support is crucial, because your awareness of the activities of your competitors and the needs of your clients and competitors are identified through other experts in your industry. Studies show that information is basically doubling every six months. It is easy to become overwhelmed by the volume and not pay attention to the important information that can have a dramatic impact on your networking and provide continual leverage to out-perform others in your respective fields.

Leads and Referrals

When you develop relationships with referral sources, you will soon find that referrals and leads are a natural part of the exchange process. Since it does take a while to build an awareness of your sources' needs, do not anticipate being able to exchange until that awareness starts to build.

As you build a relationship, you will develop a deep sense of trust between you and your sources. Just as people buy from people they know and trust, your sources will recommend you because they trust your ability to follow through on relationships professionally.

Leads are actually generated from the information assist. They are more general than referrals. Leads usually are not qualified in any way and are based upon perceived need. They are also more of a subjective understanding.

For example, if you were driving past a building with a "For Sale" sign, you can assume that there may be an opportunity for a moving company to provide services. Reading something in the newspaper about a company planning to expand to a new location would also be a lead if you do not know someone personally at that location. However, notification to your source can provide an opportunity if your source is seeking either a new sale or job potential.

When determining whether something is appropriate for your source, the best strategy is to be open and provide as much information as possible. Some people go out of their way to discover more information—to qualify the information before passing it along to their referral source. This is not necessary, however, because it is important to get the information in a timely fashion rather than take the time, perhaps on your part, to qualify it. I recommend that you provide the information that you have as soon as possible so that your sources can act on it quickly. They will qualify the information if necessary.

Stacks of books have been written on referral selling. Obtaining referrals on an ongoing basis is the objective of building any lifetime network. Yet, you should also take advantage of some of the peripheral benefits that accompany the referral. The most that you can hope for in any exchange is to be given a referral where your source has had the opportunity to identify that the other referred party's need will be met by your assistance. This qualified referral is a natural result of exchanging regularly.

This is the reason why it is so important to take advantage of exchange meetings. Gather as much information about your sources as possible and help them obtain as much information about you as possible. Exchange what you want most and what you want least in the way of referrals.

Here are some strategies for conveying concise, accurate information about your referral needs to your sources:

- Prior to a meeting, take the time to write down some of the things that you would like to accomplish during that meeting. For instance, if you are at a point where you are finding that your interests have changed, then notify your sources during that meeting. Tell your sources what you had required before and what you now need and why you've made this choice. It's always good to tell your sources why any changes have come about. Understanding your motivation, your sources will understand that the change is one that is an important one to you.

- When you start your meeting, tell your referral sources that you want to set some goals for the meeting. Then state what your goals are and have your sources state their goals. It's a good idea to call your sources prior to meetings so that they are prepared for the exchange in the same way that you are. If you call a few days in advance, your sources will have the time to draw attention to your needs with their contacts. In our busy lives, it's important to keep drawing your sources' attention back to your needs prior to a meeting.

◆ Have all your information prepared in advance, if possible. When you're prepared for the exchange, you will be able to make even greater connections. Take another look at the information once you've both transcribed it. By verbally summarizing, you may see further connections to exchange. As a result, the exchange becomes much more valuable.

When you have completed this exchange, don't forget to set another meeting date. This strategy is very similar to the impact of direct mail. In direct mail, if you do not mail continuously and at marked intervals, you will find that your impact on your target market is dramatically reduced. In fact, some experts in the direct mail field state that stopping a direct mail or direct response campaign requires you to basically begin all over again. Staying connected is key to the exchange, as is the process of creating connections within the exchange.

Creative Connections

When you focus on the different contacts or connections that you can make with others, you develop the skill of creativity. Creativity is a very important skill that utilizes cross-paradigmatic thinking. In essence, we are using both sides of our brain when we create. Both the analytical side and the creative side come together when we network, because we are making connections between what exists today and what could exist through the development of relationships.

Edward DeBono, author of the book, *Serious Creativity*, talks about creativity as lateral thinking. Most of us, DeBono says, are vertical thinkers. When we think laterally,we start to make connections that we would not otherwise be able to make. By combining the visual with the verbal or oral, we are building connections that otherwise would have been beyond our abilities.

When you create connections for other people, you are better able to understand how they create opportunities for you. Additionally, you are able to recommend how better connections can be built. The more you see it work, the more you can make it work in the future.

When one of the young associates, Scott Wattenberg, from a team within my firm first began the process of networking, he was not certain that he would be able to network effectively. His concern was that he did not know anyone and that he would not be able to make contacts that would make any difference for the firm. Through coaching, which took a relatively short period of time, Scott was able to see that his current contacts offered him the best base of new opportunities.

When Scott was able to see that he could leverage his current contacts with the firm, he started to realize that he could create opportunities. He ended up networking with someone from his girlfriend's company, which was in search of a cost-recovery software program, with a company that our firm owns that provides that type of software. When Scott saw how pleased the two parties were to be connected, he realized that the benefit of connecting two people in need of each other's assistance could help him in many ways. By creating this connection, he noticed many more connections. Every activity my associate undertook became an opportunity to create a new connection.

Within a period of two weeks, Scott ended up with two prospects and several other contacts who had a potential for being referral sources. Scott's enthusiasm for the power of networking grew dramatically. Suddenly, he could see the dynamic process of networking and how it provided an ongoing opportunity to co-create with his sources.

The whole key to creativity is understanding that you are not alone, that you can co-create opportunities with others every day. When I use the term "co-creating," it is important to understand that networking cannot be done without co-creation. You need the other contacts in order to create the connections. For the connection to be as beneficial as possible, you need to be as clear as possible regarding your needs. When you know what you want, you will get it.

Carrie Lannon now knows what she wants. After several years in advertising, Carrie realized that she very much preferred marketing. She ended up as a public relations and marketing director for a major Chicago hotel. Carrie was able to take the skills that she learned in the advertising world and apply them in a new medium. Today Carrie attributes her success in her new field to relationship building. She says that had it not been for the introspection that she did over the past several years, she would not have the clarity that she now has. Carrie adds, "it is through the development of clarity that I was able to be genuine, and through my genuineness, I was able to build rapport. This rapport created opportunities for me with any new clients that I was looking to obtain."

Carrie's journey took her to a place within that helped her build her network of quality sources. Now Carrie has access to information, resources and referrals on an ongoing basis when she wants them and how she wants them.

The skills you build in the exchange process are not difficult. They take time and sensitivity to the needs of others. Good listening skills are extremely important and enable you to identify the needs that are most important to your source. I recommend that if you think that you need to develop your listening skills, look for a class that will help you develop these skills. There is no substitute for creating connections that are based on an understood need. When you become a good listener, you become a good networker. And when you become a good networker, you end up being the recipient of a lifetime of opportunities.

Reciprocity

Every exchange involves a psychological reciprocity. Sooner or later, if you are not receiving some portion of the Five-Part Assist, you will find yourself ready to look elsewhere for better, more productive sources. If your source is not producing, then it's time to reconsider the relationship. There are relationships you will form where you anticipate something quite different than what you receive. Don't hesitate to move on to locate new sources who are more receptive.

People change. Someone who is a strong source today might not be one a month or two months from now. You never know for sure who will be your long-term sources and who will not. You will find the right people only through plenty of searching and remaining receptive to creating new relationships.

Ask for What You Want

Asking for what you want is much more difficult than it appears. We've been conditioned since childhood not to be greedy; only to ask for what we really need. But when it comes to effective networking, you can often get what you want by doing two things. First, know what you want. Through your planning, you took time to identify other work that would be most rewarding and beneficial. Now you can take that information and articulate the type of opportunities that are right for you. Everyone has different opportunities in mind:

Careerist

"I'm looking for a new position in the area of risk safety management. I want to work for a company that offers a number of benefits—especially computers for its employees."

Entrepreneur

"I'm interested in finding companies that are in need of new telecommunications systems. I want to work with companies that are expanding in value technology. These companies are not afraid to spend dollars for this important tool."

Sales Professional

"I want to find companies that are looking for new office furniture. My best prospects will be those companies who see the purchase of office furniture as an investment rather than an expense."

All of the above examples intertwine the attitudes of the purchasers and their sellers. As I mentioned before, my firm looks to do business with companies who have attitudes that "match where we're at." We call this the success attitude. Our clients are usually very entrepreneurial. They are committed to growth and show it by hiring outside consultants to assist them with their growing needs. They are committed to spending, especially on their employees. In turn, their employees out-perform other employees in other companies in their market. They achieve maximum growth in the shortest time.

The more specific you can be, the better the results. You are in control of this end of the request. If you take the time to educate your sources extensively, you will receive better results. Therefore, it is important to be as specific and as benefits-oriented as possible regarding how you help people and how others help you.

 ## Steps to Mastering the Exchange

- The core of the exchange is the creation of connections—opportunities for others and for yourself as you each explore your current contacts and resources.

- Stay open to opportunities. Enter each exchange expecting to receive and give useful *Assists.*

- Resist stagnation. Keep your exchanges challenging. Challenge yourself and your sources to continually bring more exchanges to each meeting.

- Withhold judgment. Give sources as much support during the exchanges as possible to generate the most connections.

- Educate each other. Keep working at building information to be a better source of referrals.

- Stay responsible. Ultimately, you are responsible for your own actions and your sources are responsible for theirs. You can achieve your networking goals if you commit to staying responsible. If you are not getting the results you expected, look to your actions first.

- If your source is not producing, it's time to reconsider the relationship. In some situations, what you receive is quite different than what you had anticipated. Things change; so do people.

- Understand that you will find the right people only through lots of searching through others first. Stay flexible, and you will discover that the process of qualifying becomes easier and easier each time you utilize it.

Step 5:
Leveraging Your
Best Sources

Once you've developed your referral source base, you have begun to build a MegaNetwork. Your next challenge is finding ways to introduce yourself and your products and services to decision makers—prospects or employers. Begin by building relationships with the inside or outside influencers who know decision makers. Many decision makers ask for impressions from their inside staffs (inside influencers) and outside consultants (outside influencers) when considering a new product, service or potential employee. The more people who know you *and* think favorably of you, the better your chances of getting a new job or landing a new account.

Leveraging your best sources means building strong relationships with a select few. This involves networking *vertically* rather than *horizontally*. When you network vertically, you develop relationships with key influencers whose networks reach both *wide* and *deep*. The initial

stages of networking—meeting and greeting contacts—
have almost become opiates for the masses. In the last
five years, as networking has become a national and perhaps international buzzword, many people still have different understandings of what it means to them.

Horizontal networking often involves casual conversation with minimal potential for results other than further conversations. Vertical networking changes the concept of networking into a relationship development skill
that maximizes current contacts to leverage new sources
and new prospects.

When you network vertically, you appreciate the
quality of the relationship versus the number or quantity
of the people that you contact. No longer are you back in
the '80s looking at the ratio between the number of
people you contact and the resulting number of prospects that you acquire. Instead, you are seeking to leverage a relationship to obtain maximum potential for the
exchange of highly qualified referrals.

As a vertical networker, you mine an opportunity or
relationship to discover things you might never have
learned. You value every comment and every meeting
that you have with your contacts. When you appreciate
others through the vertical relationship, you begin to see
the depth of one's interaction with others in a short
period of time. It is amazing how many new contacts,
referral sources and prospects one party can develop
within a few days. When you network through referral
source meetings, you'll be surprised by the dynamic
growth of your network on a day by day basis. You will
experience the exponential power of quality networking.

People who have participated in quantity sales often
have trouble adjusting to a different type of relationship
to build sales opportunities. If you fit that description, be
assured that your awareness of a difference in the relationship building process will enable you to acquire

much more within a very short period of time. Mega-Networking is not about marketing or sales in the traditional sense, it's about a new way to create opportunities.

When you merit the respect and appreciation of a referral source, you have built a strong vertical relationship that will outdistance any number of shallow encounters.

Leveraging

Leveraging is a process that enables people to network beyond their circle of familiarity to reach influential sources. It allows you to network vertically.

Recently, I spoke with a regional sales manager of a Fortune 500 company who was concerned that her sales reps were missing many opportunities to increase their current sales closures. As she put it, "We're all over the place. We don't create an environment where we can build relationships."

The sales manager was also concerned that once these reps made sales, they ignored the best introduction to new customers—referrals from their current customers. In other words, this manager's reps were focusing on getting the quick sale, rather than building relationships for repeat buying opportunities.

The quick sale is the ultimate deceiver, because it lulls you into thinking that you have achieved the best result. But the results you achieve are much less than would be possible with the multiple sales effect of leveraging.

The whole strategy here is to nurture the relationship in order to create an environment for repeat business. When you create referral sources, you build a repeat business conduit.

Leverage your current referral sources, one introduction after another, to more qualified prospects. During your exchanges, you can ask for these introductions. You can also educate your sources to make sure that they introduce you efficiently. From one new opportunity to the next, you will find the quality of your network improving. You will come to know what you want by constantly challenging yourself to identify the best leads and referrals.

Treat your referral sources as your best prospects, because they'll lead you to these prospects. Ask for referrals when you've created bridges of trust. A nonintrusive way to seek referrals is to ask "Who else do you know who could benefit from what I have to offer?"

Once you achieve a bridge of trust between you and your referral source, you have developed a climate that is perfect for exchange. Your exchanges will get more and more productive, and you will find that you are the recipient of excellent leads and referrals, information and continuous promotional support. You will find that it is easier for you to have your source's name on the tip of your tongue whenever you meet new people, and you will know just the right words to use to connect others to your sources.

How To Nurture Your Referral Sources

- *Meet in person.*   Arrange to meet in person as often as possible. There is no substitute for a face-to-face meeting. Take the time to arrange a convenient spot to exchange on a regular basis. Meetings that are prearranged to fall on the same day of the month at the same time ultimately become the most effective process you can use.

- *Rank the degree of influence.*   Don't forget to continually measure the degree of influence your sources have with others. This introduces a quantitative measurement system into the qualitative process of networking. For instance, if your source says that his/her influence with a particular prospect is at a Level 4, you can count on a very favorable introduction to this prospect.

This technique is very effective and should not be perceived as intrusive. It actually provides a substantive system for decreasing the effort and time required to build new relationships for both parties in the exchange. Here's how it works:

- *Meet and then exceed the needs of your referral sources.* Find out what your sources needs are and what motivates them, then meet and exceed those needs.

- *Ask, ask and then, ask some more.* Keep asking questions that help you get a better understanding of who knows the decision makers you want to reach, then ask for introductions and referrals.

- *Deliver a quality service or product.* Networking will not develop new career opportunities or land you a great account if you don't deliver what you say you can. Stay technically and personally sharp.

When you leverage, you focus on project collaborations and strategic alliances. You work at maximizing your existing relationships so that both you and your sources take advantage of all the hard work you've done before you met each other.

The Path to Achievement

MegaNetworking keeps you connected with your relationships. By helping others connect with those who can help them, you leverage a minimum amount of time into a maximum number of benefits over and over and over again. Your genuine interest in the success of others will ultimately be your path to success.

When everyone contributes a small amount, the result is a cumulative benefit equal to much more than the sum of its parts. When you educate others about your success, they can follow in your footsteps, taking a path toward achievement. Realize that it's okay to promote yourself. By letting others know your abilities, and by sharing those abilities with others, you will be perceived as a competent, qualified partner. Those individuals who pat themselves on the back for others to merely praise on a continuous basis are quite different from proactive people who say, "I'm good at what I do, and I'd like to share my talent with you," and "I appreciate you and I wish that you'd tell me what your talents are and share them with me."

Another good example of leveraging comes from the organization where I work. We have a team that focuses on the health care industry called FERS KMR, led by Doug Smith. Interested in working with dentists, Doug was aware that there are some nuances involved with acquiring business in that field. Doug assigned Diane Smith—a hygienist by profession—to identify dental practices that needed help building both better management and operational structures.

Diane had difficulty building a client base with this group. In analyzing the situation, Doug found that the perceived impression of Diane was one of lack of influence because she was a hygienist and not a dentist. However, in re-strategizing and focusing on the concept of leverage, Diane began to approach other dental hygienists who were insiders and had influence with the dentists. As a result, Diane was able to accomplish her original goal: acquiring new accounts with dental practices. Because the dentists trusted their relationships with their dental hygienists, there was a natural bridge of influence between the hygienist and the dentist. This bridge, when connected on the other side to relationships

Diane built among the hygienists, developed a much more effective way of achieving a communication conduit to the dentists. Diane's efforts, which began with the dental hygienists and led to follow-up introductions to the dentists, allowed her to accomplish her goal in a much shorter period of time.

Identifying Influencers

When the relationship you choose to build is one of meeting someone with a current higher span of influence, don't be discouraged. Realize that there are other entrees to these people through those who influence them. There are many proactive influencers who understand the power of the exchange—or will understand once educated.

Look at your market. Take time to identify the influencers. In the legal market, the paralegals or court clerks could be influencers with the attorneys—or vice versa. In corporate America, influencers could be gatekeepers, secretaries, middle managers, senior executives. In the not-for-profit world, influencers could be volunteers or the people who sit on boards.

Seek out proactive people who are interested in a mutual exchange. Working hard at obtaining/building relationships with people who are not open to this type of process is counterproductive to your plan to build a MegaNetwork. Don't waste your time with disinterested parties.

When leveraging a network opportunity, you will find that a series of exchanges creates a ripple of more exchanges. Don't make the mistake of building off of difficult relationships. Later you'll feel sorry for yourself because the majority of your relationships are with difficult people. However, if you take the time to plan up front, you will find that you can acquire a small base of powerful, influential, agreeable people who will take the initiative to help you build your network. In turn, they will introduce you to other proactive people—and so on, and so on. Why make it harder for yourself than it has to be? A small amount of planning can result in an enormous gain.

At its heart, leveraging is the process of maximizing your efforts. You no longer have to worry all the time about whether what you want will be achieved. You will start to see the potential and the power of leveraging as you build awareness through your relationships. The continuous quality that will result from regularly scheduled meetings—whether they're in person or by phone—will ultimately generate one opportunity after another. But you must begin with that end in mind and find those individuals who will be partners in creating opportunities.

If you are new to an industry or new to a marketplace, you've still had a number of years of building relationships with your family members and friends. And those people have influence on other people—their parents, friends they've had, people they've met throughout their lives. Even younger people can lead you to others who are seasoned in their various industries. Ask for one introduction after another, and constantly be aware of what you have to offer in return.

Your appreciation of another person's assistance and a commitment to try to give something back in the future will be adequate compensation for them. Realize that what you perceive would be an equal exchange is often much more than others really want, especially those who sincerely enjoy mentoring. Their exchange allows them to provide assistance similar to what they had received before—perhaps in their earlier years—from their own mentors. Sources give to you willingly, knowing that you will keep up the chain of giving—supporting—mentoring—MegaNetworking.

Steps to Leveraging Your Best Sources

- ◆ Continuously look for both inside and outside influencers who know the decision makers you want to meet. These influencers will help you achieve a stronger potential for doing business with or obtaining jobs from the decision makers.

- ◆ Turn your focus from quantity to quality in order to maximize the power of leveraging.

- ◆ Use your strongest relationships first to achieve your goals. Through leveraging, you can work from the strength these relationships hold within their circles of influence to gain entry to the decision makers you wish to meet.

- ◆ Leveraging enables you to quickly move from one influential source to the next.

8

Step 6:
Managing the Four
Levels of Your
Network

Once you begin to acquire the quantity that evolves from a quality base of referral sources, you'll find yourself with an entirely new problem—managing the four levels of the networking matrix. Remember, your focus is on *quality*. You need to immediately simplify the process of generating and managing quality referrals. The following strategies can help you streamline your MegaNetworking System:

1. *Staying connected: the problem of the cooling Rolodex*
    How long should you wait between calls? I know people who have set up referral source meetings anywhere from every week to every other week to once a month. I recommend starting out, if you can, on an every other week basis. There are many

Figure 8.1   Networking Levels Matrix

Level 1 Baseline Networking	Level 2 Strategic Networking	Level 3 Referral Source Networking	Level 4 Mega- Networking
Networking Groups	Industry Niches	Leveraging	Cross-Level Networking
Organiza- tion Meet- ings	Networking Plans	Five-Part Assists	Strategic Alliances
Friends, Relatives	Qualifying Processes	Scheduled Meetings/ Structured Exchanges	Project Collabora- tions

people who do not have the time to meet with someone every other week. Discuss what would be convenient for both of you, but make sure that you meet at least once a month.

Make use of new and better ways to keep in touch with simple but effective tools, such as postcards. Today's postcards are of high quality and often achieve the same result as a letter with much less effort and cost.

When you complement your verbal correspondence with written correspondence, you build stronger bridges of trust between you and your referral sources. This further accelerates the growth of your relationships.

2. *Stay structured.* It is important to have a series of *consistent exchanges.* Try to establish a set time for your meetings, for example—on the third Thursday or the second Tuesday of each month. Or, if you are meeting every other week, set an exact time, such as every other Tuesday or Thursday. This structure will enable both you and your source to *anticipate* and therefore *prepare* for your next exchange. Once you've developed a pattern, which usually takes about three meetings, you will have a solid structure that generates the optimum environment for the exchange to be as effective as possible.

3. *Stay aware.* As the world becomes more and more customer service oriented, there is an increased demand for quality service. Marketing research specialist John Lytle puts it this way, "Today's excellence is tomorrow's mediocrity." Continue to focus your attention on relationships as our country grows more globally active. The information explosion will spawn an increase in service jobs. Those who are aware and proactive will excel. Those who have strong interpersonal skills will find unlimited opportunities. To participate in endless opportunities, always follow the rules of networking etiquette. When you have meetings, be on time. When you say you're going to follow through, do so. When you come to a meeting, be prepared. Respect the time you both have taken to meet with one another. The return on your investment of time and effort will pay off more quickly and strongly than ever before.

4. *Use your Referral Source Meeting Summaries.* Try to keep up with your summaries. They will help you and your referral sources see and experience the benefits of building some structure around

what would otherwise be very casual relationships. Without the structure, the relationship will
not grow as quickly and effectively. It will turn into
more of a serendipitous event without preparation, without any goals and with fewer results.

5. *Have Fun.*   Your exchanges can be times when you
   really enjoy one another's company. The exchange
   does not have to be focused primarily on business.
   I have often arrived to meet with a source and the
   topic of conversation was a problem that I was
   having at home with my children or a situation that
   I was concerned about with someone I was coaching. Your sources tend to become your confidants,
   and you find that you have the great benefit of
   being able to be honest and vulnerable with them.
   Sharing that vulnerability is also important to creating rapport. Both parties will be the beneficiaries
   of one another's care and concern. To assume that
   you will not find yourselves in any state other than
   maximum efficiency when you exchange is not
   realistic. There will be times when you will feel like
   you would like to do anything other than meet
   with someone. It will be at those times that you will
   truly benefit from having another human being
   who cares about and trusts you.

6. *Prioritize.*   Use your Referral Source Meeting Summaries and the "To-Do" list you created for commitments that you made between exchanges. Follow through on your priorities. Continue to prioritize other networking activities throughout the
   month. When you talk with your sources and you
   get pieces of information—perhaps in between
   meetings—ask, "Which one would you recommend
   as most important to do first?" Continually realize
   that no matter what you do, you will be making
   trade-offs. You will also receive unexpected referrals, leads and pieces of information. Keep deciding

what is the first, second, third, etc., most important thing to do. These decisions will become easier as you come to know yourself and your goals better. Those unexpected pieces of information will be placed on the same pile with the same importance as everything you must do, unless you take a few moments to prioritize.

7. *Set aside one day a week or one hour a day to follow up.* For instance, if you set aside every Friday morning or if you call people at a particular time each day, this will help you feel less frustrated. You can contact people and say, "Please contact me between 3:00 P.M. and 4:00 P.M. today," or "You can contact me between 3:00 P.M. and 4:00 P.M. each day." You must have a time when people can return your call, and you certainly must have a time when you can return their calls. This benefits you by managing those unexpected calls. When you do get them, say, "This is not a convenient time. However, I usually receive calls between 3:00 P.M. and 4:00 P.M. each day," or whatever time works for you.

8. *Know your down times.* Become aware of those times when you are not at your highest performance level and work around them. Utilize those times to do work that is not a high priority, when you are not presenting yourself to others. When people do encounter you—either by telephone or in person—you are performing at your maximum potential.

9. *Keep your referral source base small.* The secret to building or managing a network is to start with the strategic network where you have, at most, five to ten referral sources. Do not overlook the other elements of the Five-Part Assist. For example, there might be someone who is not at liberty to provide

you with referrals—such as attorneys who have certain ethical restrictions—but they can offer a wealth of inside information on the markets that you are interested in approaching.

The strategic network is to the MegaNetwork what a good car would be to its owner. Just as a good car will take you from where you are now to where you want to go, a good referral source can take you from cold calling to top level networking. Where the car provides all of the parts for steering and moving in one direction or another, the referral source becomes the guide who will assist you in moving in the direction that you would like to travel. The physical structure of the car is like the structure of the exchange.

Many times I have gone into a client's office and found overstuffed Rolodexes or tall stacks of business cards bound together by rubber bands. I ask them, "Do you keep in touch with all of those people?" They look at their cards in a bewildered manner and return to me saying, "No. I have a problem with that." And yet, these are the same people who are constantly networking, asking about the next event or the next person they can meet. Their actions are similar to what is sometimes called the *Cinderella Syndrome*. These networkers are hoping that the prince will be at the ball. Like everyone else, you are probably eternally hopeful that you will discover just the right people to help you by buying your service or products or hiring you, but it is very unlikely. Rather, through the strategic marketing and sales activities developed via MegaNetworking, you can find and be introduced to the people that you hope to meet.

One of the best ways to manage is to decide ahead of time what you will and will not do. If given a lead or referral that you decide you don't want, be honest. Refer the opportunity to someone who would be willing and able to take it. The person to whom you pass the lead or referral will appreciate the contact and more than likely take the time to reciprocate at a future date.

10. *Focus on Creating Introductions.* Make sure to ask your referral sources to introduce you to someone you've been wanting to meet. The Introduction is a key strategy for managing your network.

    You might ask your referral source something like this—"You said that Mr. Y at ABC Corporation would be the decision maker. Do you know Mr. Y?" (If the source does know Mr. Y, ask "Would there be the opportunity to introduce me to him at some particular event that he might be attending?") Remember, it's always more effective to meet in person and when people attend events, they're anticipating being introduced to people they have not met before. It is a much better environment because of that anticipation and social atmosphere.

    However, if there is no chance of a face-to-face introduction, you could ask, "Would you mind giving Mr. Y a call to ask him if he would be receptive to my coming to speak with him for five minutes for an information-gathering interview?"

    If your source does not know Mr. Y, you could ask, "Who do you know at ABC Corporation?" You are looking for inside influencers who know the decision maker. But you won't know the *degree* of influence these insiders have until you have a conversation. Remember, the purpose of an exchange with any of these people is to first gather information. Inside influencers are talking to you because they have an existing relationship with your source.

Stay respectful of their time, and they will help you build a strong base of information on the company and its decision makers *before* you meet them. This additional assistance can well mean a new customer, client or job. Therefore, the more information you can gather from a number of inside sources, the better prepared you will be to match the company's needs with your skills.

Effective Management Starts with Communication

Michael Schrage, the author of *Shared Minds, The New Technologies of Collaboration* and a specialist in the area of collaboration, has found that most misunderstandings and disputes derive from three main sources. These three areas are: personal positions, unstated assumptions and unstated criteria.

When managing your relationships, you must first manage the effectiveness of your communications. For instance, a 15-minute conversation could be trimmed down to 5 minutes once you develop an understanding of the techniques for building good communication skills. Be aware that people have their own positions on things. Rather than assume what these positions are, ask.

There are a number of general questions that you can ask regarding someone's personal position. For example, find out how, with whom, when and why your sources network.

All of these questions will help you better understand how your sources process the information they receive from others and how they build relationships. This will make you more effective in building relationships in a way that complements the natural style of those with whom you will interact.

Schrage's discovery provides a foundation for accelerating the exchange and achieving better results faster. Here are some ways to implement Schrage's theories immediately:

- *Personal positions and unstated assumptions* When questioning others regarding their personal positions, also look for assumptions that they have made. Their assumptions come from their current awareness. As you develop stronger relationships using the MegaNetworking System, you will learn more about the personal opinions of sources and the assumptions they made to create these opinions. You will also learn a lot about how people behave as compared to what they think about how they behave.

  For example, there are many people who state that they are against violence on television and yet, according to statistics, many of these same people watch violent programs daily. Look for your sources' personal positions based on what they *do* rather than what they *say*. Some people will say that they will do many things for you in order to get you new business or help you find a job. Yet, each time you talk with them, these people have an excuse as to why they have not done anything yet. I recommend that if you are promised something that is not delivered more than twice, you should choose to refocus your attention on others with more follow-through.

  There are fewer people who will follow through, but again, by asking, "Who is the best networker out there (in a particular area or organization)?" and "Why?" you may find someone who is open and proactive. You will meet these people and be introduced, or ask to be introduced to these people, so you will not have to look for them.

- ◆ Unstated *criteria* are almost totally eliminated with the creation of Referral Source Meetings and Meeting Summaries. You will avoid many misunderstandings, because the summaries will point out to you on a consistent basis that networking is a two-way street.

Be honest with your sources. For example, as mentioned before, if you are unable to provide referrals for one reason or another, make sure that your source knows this and understands what that means to the exchange. When unstated information is presented up front, you will discover that there is great value to what does exist in the relationship, and you will be building that, addressing one problem after another and trying to resolve them. You will move from waiting for new opportunities to occur to making them happen.

Managing Smart

You need to determine a good place to store your key contacts, your referral sources and your prospects. Some people store this information in a notebook with tabs that help you alphabetize by last name. If you wish to cross-reference, you can also separate the information by company names. You may find it useful to store your information in a Rolodex or file box. Or, if you travel on electronic highways, you can enter your information into an electronic database. Contact management programs are gaining in popularity as more and more people use them to manage their networks.

The contact management program that I utilize is Symantec's *ACT!* I find it easy to transfer information from one person to another through ACT! I use it to keep names of people I read about and hear about as well as those I've met.

Whatever system you use, maintain it regularly. When someone mentions a person in a particular field whom you should know about, jot that person's name down. Make a point of finding out more about that person and either contacting him or her directly or at least building information on that contact for a future exchange.

With all your contacts and sources, continually ask: "What connection can I make with this person? What might I offer? What might he or she offer?" Ask this with an eye to the networking matrix. "How can I create a third-level or fourth-level networking opportunity?" The more you focus on what you can do together, the faster you will see results.

When you are trying to reach another general contact to further qualify the potential of their becoming either prospects or referral sources, the best strategy is to schedule a telephone conversation. The alternative is to schedule a face-to-face meeting. The result you are seeking is to access these people without constantly playing telephone tag. One of the best strategies for making this contact is to call the person you wish to reach and leave a message with them (which will probably be on their voice mail). You might say, "Sue, I was referred to you by so and so and I would love to have a chance to talk with you. Would next Thursday or Friday at 10:00 A.M. be a better time?"

Time Management

Good time management skills are essential. You can either maximize your time by organizing and prioritizing your everyday tasks, or you can approach each day in a completely reactionary mode. The latter approach will result in unanticipated problems taking too long, as well as a feeling of frustration because you consistently find that you cannot accomplish what you hope to do. How-

ever, there are many different ways to organize and prioritize your daily work life. A great networker who also
happens to be an organizational skills coach, Thalia Poulos,
author of the booklet, *Total Quality Organization (TQO)*,
emphasizes *self-management* over *time management.* Effective self-management is based on discipline. Self-management starts with knowing what you want and then
disciplining yourself to stay committed to your goals.

The areas that you want to organize include:

- *Reading.*   Set aside time for reading by storing
  reading materials in a prearranged place. A special
  basket or container is a good idea. This container
  can be retrieved during a daily quiet time. By
  taking reflective time to read, you will be better
  prepared to deal with life's everyday challenges
  Also, taking the time to read inspirational books
  and ideas is an important means of keeping yourself focused.

  The time you take to read, journal or reflect will
  help you plan your next series of activities. By
  removing yourself from making decisions during
  or before a problem arises, you more readily anticipate the outcome of those problems. You also have
  additional options for working through problem
  times in a proactive, rather than a defensive or
  reactive, manner.

- *Correspondence.*   Save time on correspondence by
  creating several letters that can be used as templates
  for future letters. One letter could be a sales or
  cover letter for a particular industry. Another could
  be a follow-up thank you letter. A template for a
  proposal is also wise to allow you to quickly fill
  in the blanks or add to it as necessary. Keep effective phrases—especially beginnings and endings
  of letters—stored in your computer. Collect different letters and books that you find effective. Check

your local library and bookstore for books that showcase sample letters and phrases. Two examples are *Words that Sell* by Richard Boyan and *Letters that Sell* by Edward Werz.

Another way to build effective correspondence is to create scripts of good verbal responses to questions that you might get asked during telephone conversations. For example, I once had a script that listed a variety of objections that people might make when I was selling a particular consulting service. By creating a script ahead of time, I was able to address in a proactive way any objections made by my potential clients. The scripts were very helpful in developing comfort with the words that could be used to avoid sounding defensive, when a particular concern was called to my attention. By developing scripts, practicing them ahead of time and continuously listening for specific phrases from people presenting objections, I built a file of concise, positively powerful responses to each objection.

It takes the development of good habits to generate the ease, enthusiasm and genuineness that you will need to effectively sell yourselves, your products or your services.

- *Projects.* Keep packets of information about yourself, whether it's your resume or sales literature, in a convenient location. Setting aside five to ten packets is helpful in keeping you efficient when someone asks you to send them information about you or your company.

- *Telephone calls.* Keep a separate telephone correspondence log either electronically or manually. Check off the calls you have responded to, and note any further action you should take in reference to each call.

Trade-Ups

The ongoing benefits of prioritizing and scheduling your time for activities that help you prepare for unexpected situations will bring about a sense of confidence that working spontaneously will not. Planning and prioritizing your activities require you to get in touch with what you should do first, second, third, etc. Your priorities will change continuously, and by constantly adjusting your priorities, you get more in touch with what you really want. Realize that life is a series of experiences that either allow you to choose beforehand those things that are most important to you or, if you don't plan, force you to choose in reaction to something outside of your control.

Every day you make trade-offs, or as I prefer to call them, *trade-ups*. You trade-up to something you want to do more from something you want to do less. When I began prioritizing, for example, I found that writing was extremely important to me. I realized that I had to set time aside for writing because that time was not going to be made for me. When I made time to write, other things became less important.

As you determine the things that are most important to you, you will experience similar results. By continuously prioritizing, you will discover that you also become better at knowing what you want.

 ## Steps to Managing the Four Levels of Your Network

- *Prioritize.*   When you prioritize, you streamline your daily activities, which over time enables you to accomplish your goals much more quickly.

Figure 8.2 Exercises for Prioritizing

1. Name three things that you would like to have more time for (in order of priority, of course!)

    1._____

    2._____

    3._____

2. What is keeping you from re-prioritizing your sched-ule to take time for these priorities?

    _____

    _____

    _____

    _____

3. Where could you possibly take time—15 minutes here, 20 minutes there—on a consistent basis? List the days and time slots that you are committing to create time for your priorities.

    Day _____   Time _____
    Day _____   Time _____
    Day _____   Time _____
    Day _____   Time _____
    Day _____   Time _____

- *Stay connected.*   Never leave a good contact or referral source without setting up the next meeting. This way you won't lose contact and will naturally create a strong bridge of communication and continuous opportunities.

- *Use the Referral Source Meeting Summaries.*   These summaries help you take advantage of the many opportunities that come from exchanging with others.

- *Be picky.*   Don't try to do everything. Always look for the things that will have the strongest potential for *Assists.*

- *Less is more.*   Always take time for quality relationships, but limit your time for those you recognize as not valuable.

- *Optimize.*   If you spend all your time with relationships that are mutually beneficial, you won't have any time for relationships that don't work.

9

Group Therapy:
Finding and Forming
Groups that Produce
Healthy Leads

There has been an explosion of networking groups over the past five years. From job support groups to owner's forums to industry specific associations to leads groups—where noncompeting businesses pass leads and referrals on a regular basis—networking has become a way of life for thousands. Networking groups are here to stay, and more and more will be starting all the time. Ask around for the best groups for your industry. And look to general resources like the *Encyclopedia of Associations* (available at your library) for a comprehensive list of associations and networking groups around the country.

Tom Camden's books—*How to Get a Job in Chicago, How to Get a Job in New York*, etc.—are excellent resources if you are looking for jobs and/or associations in different major cities around the United States. My first book,

The Chicago Entrepreneur's Sourcebook has listings of associations, an overview of the economic climate of the area and a comprehensive listing of government organizations that offer low-cost or no-cost information assistance. Supplement these books by reading your local newspapers and magazines for listings of local networking events.

Creating Your Own Group

If you choose to create your own networking group, the following steps will help you avoid some of the pitfalls that I have seen other groups encounter:

1. *Decide the purpose of the group.*   Is the group's purpose to simply exchange information, such as an owners' or executives' support group? Will you exchange leads and referrals like in a leads group? With a leads group, the objective is to obtain and give quality leads and referrals. I recommend looking at the type of leads and referrals you need and building your group around that type of exchange.

   Exclusivity is something that most leads groups uphold. Here, only one person is allowed to represent a particular business category. This person will receive all the leads and referrals generated by the group's members for that category. For instance, if the member is a moving company, all the leads for movers would go to that company. Another mover would not be allowed to enter the group. However, if there is a difference between two movers—one performs only commercial moving while the other does only residential moving—you might allow both of them to be in the group. Some groups allow the initial member to decide whether to allow the potential member's participation. Other groups include potential members in the decision making

Figure 9.1 Creating a Network Group

What follows is a model for creating a networking group. Use this information as a guide to form your own group.

General Overview

The Executive Network is a networking group dedicated to maximizing your time and resources to achieve good business referrals. The success of the group is monitored in dollars transacted.

The Executive Network is a formalized group with no more than 30 noncompeting businesses or professionals. We meet weekly to exchange quality referrals. The amount of business transacted among members will be tabulated monthly.

Objectives of the group include making valuable business contacts, sharing information and forming working partnerships. Networking in the group is a cooperative process that results in both professional and personal gains. The Executive Network offers a valuable marketing and advertising service dedicated to increasing financial business success for the entrepreneur or professional.

Who Can Become a Member?

- Entrepreneurs, small business owners, key employees
- Decision makers
- Professionals
- Sales representatives

Note: The Network is designed to create financial business success through networking. Individuals who currently do business by referrals, cold calling or expensive advertising and marketing pieces will find The Network to be a less costly, less time intensive and more effective way to do business.

Guests

Each group is limited to 30 noncompeting business members. Members may bring guests to the meetings. If there is an open business category within the group and a guest wishes to become a member, the guest should contact the group leader who will complete the membership application.

Guests are allowed to attend one group meeting prior to committing to membership. They can participate fully in the meeting and are subject to the same limitations as members.

Members are encouraged to bring guests as long as there are openings within the group. This will ensure the group's continuous growth and stability.

process. Some groups require a unanimous vote, while others will allow a majority vote.

2. *Build a group around a similar target market.* For example, if you are in a business market and you are targeting companies between $1 million and $15 million in sales, you might create a group that targets a similar market. In this group, therefore, you would not have a member who is targeting a consumer market, such as a residential real estate professional.

3. *Limit the number of members in your group.* More than 30 members will take away from the sharing environment necessary for effective networking. You can also look at forming smaller groups. For example, a printer, a graphic designer, a free-lance writer, a public relations specialist and an advertising agency may form one synergistic sub-group. Such a group would have the strongest potential of meeting with companies that would be interested in their combined services. You would also have the potential to give more leads and referrals within a small sub-group, because you would have more in-depth knowledge of *how* to sell the services of your other group members.

4. *Develop a method for tracking leads and referrals.* Whether your group is informal or formal, you should have some type of tracking system so that you can see the benefits that are developed through networking. Consider developing a networking matrix. Below you will see a sample of a matrix that you might use to see who gave what and got what in the networking group and thereby assess whether this group is a beneficial group in which to remain and participate. Realize, however, that it will take at least three months before you can adequately determine the worth of a group.

Figure 9.2 Networking Matrix

From ___/___/___   **To** ___/___/___
(Two, Four, Six-Week Period, etc.)

	John Gave	Ann Gave	Jill Gave	Henry Gave
John Got	-- --	5 leads 2 referrals	5 leads 1 referral	3 leads 1 referral
Ann Got	2 leads 1 referral	-- --	3 leads 2 referrals	3 leads 2 referrals
Jill Got	4 leads 2 referrals	3 leads 1 referral	-- --	5 leads 2 referals
Henry Got	1 lead 4 referrals	2 leads 3 referrals	4 leads 1 referral	-- --

5. *Arrange one-on-one meetings with members between group meetings.* One-on-one meetings will help you to build a more intimate rapport with your members and allow you to assess more quickly the benefits of staying in the group. Efforts by the members will be reflected through the dollars that are transacted by individuals in the group.

In Chicago, GONE (the Greater O'Hare Networking Executives) has been very effective in utilizing a networking matrix for their very successful group. GONE members exchange millions of dollars of business annually. You, too, can achieve this success if you get proactive members who are committed to helping one another. Try also to locate members who have networks that reach both wide and deep. And, make sure that these people are not already over-committed to giving their leads and referrals to others.

6. *Set up bylaws for your group.*   There will be times when you find that you have a member who is not giving his or her fair share of leads and referrals. It is good to set up rules ahead of time concerning the requirements of membership. Create a set of bylaws that set forth what will and will not be acceptable to the group. Issues you might include in the bylaws are: the number of meetings you may miss, (many groups allow three consecutive absences before you no longer have rights as a member), the number of referrals or leads you are required to bring to each meeting and requirements of running the meeting (for example, having each member take a turn at running the meeting).

From time to time, there will be members who just do not fit into the group. In one group that I created, we developed a standard where potential members were invited to one meeting by a member. A vote was then taken among current members to determine/screen whether the potential member would fit into the group. If the potential member was not accepted, it was the responsibility of the member who first invited the potential member to notify him or her.

7. *Meeting Times.*   Some people like to meet every other week, while others prefer weekly or monthly meetings. It is the decision of the group by either a majority or unanimous vote to determine the most equitable meeting schedule.

In running your meetings, keep to an agenda. All members should know through timelines on the

---

Figure 9.3 Sample Weekly Meeting Agenda

I. Arrival

A. Registration

B. Informal networking

C. Breakfast buffet

D. Seating

(20 minutes)

II. Group Leader Introduction

A. Announcements/general

B. Number of referrals given and received

C. Total dollars transacted so far in the group

D. Old business

E. New business

F. Open discussion

(10 minutes)

III. Full Room Networking / Introductions

A. Each member to give a 30-second introduction of his or her business or profession

---

agenda, the status of each event. For example, from 8:00 A.M. to 8:15 A.M., introductions are made—a 15-second to 30-second introduction for each person. The meeting will then move on to another 30 minute segment—between 8:15 A.M. and 8:45 A.M.—during which leads are shared among members. Many networking groups then have what are known as *craft talks* where a member provides a special presentation about his or her business.

8. *When it's time to move on.* There will come a time when members choose to leave the group for one reason or another. People move, things change, people change and make transitions to other opportunities or career paths. When you find that you can no longer give or are no longer motivated to provide business to others in the group, it will benefit all concerned if you leave. If you decide to leave a networking group, attempt to maintain a strong relationship with the membership.

Group Dynamics

Every group has its own special personality. I have found that there are many networkers who join multiple groups. When you form your own group, ask questions about the number of networking affiliations a potential member has. Be careful. Some people are very active networkers, but the number of referrals they can provide or the number of people you may be in competition with when you receive a referral from them may become a problem.

Some networking groups charge several thousand dollars a year or more and others are free or charge a nominal fee. Usually groups combine their meeting with some type of meal, and the meal becomes an additional charge above and beyond the meeting cost.

Leads groups exist across the country, and area Chambers of Commerce often sponsor such groups. The local newspaper is a good source for locating local groups, as well as a good resource to use when advertising the formation of a new group. For low-cost publicity, send a press-release announcement to the media. The one-page release should list the what, when, where, why and how of the group and a telephone number for interested parties to call.

Some groups provide ongoing educational support for their members. They provide specialists who give workshops or speeches on items of common interest to their members. Many people enjoy the additional benefits of receiving continuing education along with new business opportunities.

Many job support groups are forming through local libraries and religious institutions. Check with the institutions that interest you to see if they have support groups.

Other groups focus on support for personal interests and needs. Many of them are good places to meet referral sources. A colleague of mine networks with the hockey members he coaches. Every Saturday for six months out of the year, he coaches a team of amateur hockey enthusiasts. They build skills, relieve stress and have fun while playing as a team.

There are also many volunteer associations that offer opportunities for professionals to meet and share skills while working on a worthy cause, such as working with the United Way or some other not-for-profit organization. These associations give you the opportunity to interact with and learn from fellow board members

Such groups can be good places to gather new skills or sharpen old skills when your daily work life does not provide those opportunities.

10

Top-Level Networking

When you are *top-level networking*, you are reversing your networking strategy. Instead of working the bottom of the networking matrix, you are working Levels 3 and 4. Spend 80 percent of your marketing time on activities at these levels. How do you stay at the top? Here are the actions that you need to take on a constant basis:

- ◆ Know the trends.
- ◆ Know the influencers in your industry.
- ◆ Know the influencers in your community.
- ◆ Know the businesses in your target market.
- ◆ Know your competition.
- ◆ Know the internal influencers in your targeted companies.
- ◆ Know the external influencers in your targeted companies.

Figure 10.1   Networking Levels Matrix

Level 1 Baseline Networking	Level 2 Strategic Networking	Level 3 Referral Source Networking	Level 4 Mega-Networking
Networking Groups	Industry Niches	Leveraging	Cross-Level Networking
Organization Meetings	Networking Plans	Five-Part Assists	Strategic Alliances
Friends, Relatives	Qualifying Processes	Scheduled Meetings/ Structured Exchanges	Project Collaborations

Long-Term Success

Long-term success is more about attitude than anything else. In our *get-it-now* society, it's easy to develop a short-term mentality. This starts when we are in school. When we took classes, completed homework assignments, sweated over finals and then left everything behind a mere four months later, we were grateful to end our short-term projects and move on to the next class. Having carried these short-term expectations into our adult years, we often find ourselves struggling to stay committed to relationships. Sometimes, we apply instant expectations to our networking and concentrate on quick results.

In order to shift the focus from immediate gratification to long-term success, concentrate on Levels 3 and 4 of the matrix. Additionally, make the actions in the above list an important part of your daily networking activities.

Begin this process by reading with a focus on people rather than events. Read everything from magazines to newspapers. Stay connected with the world. Ask questions of everyone you meet. Ask what connections they have: What influencers do they know? Where do they usually network? What associations do they belong to or are they happy with? When asking these questions, give people time to make a connection from one person to the next. Here's what MegaNetworker Polly Pancoe, of Hotel Management Resource in Chicago, has to say about building relationships:

> As a fan for over 25 years, of 'Doc' Severinsen, I recently spoke to him after a wonderful performance with the Milwaukee Symphony Orchestra. We started discussing different Chicago hotels, which was my expertise as the president of a hotel reservation company. Doc was lamenting the closing of one of his favorite Chicago hotels where he had performed for many years. I offered some suggestions of good second choices for him. I was thrilled when I was able to offer my assistance to someone who had provided me with many great performances. What I realized was that even though 'Doc' had many connections in his industry, I was able to be instrumental in assisting him in a town where he had contacts, but not as many or as strong as I had.

Entrepreneurs

A key strategy for bringing in new business and obtaining repeat sales is to build a base of marketing information on your prospects. This helps you avoid the problem of finding yourself without sales opportunities between projects. By building a database of top prospects and customers who would like to purchase your products or services, you will be able to leverage your marketing efforts to influence these people quickly and effectively.

Figure 10.2   Gathering Information

Whether you are a careerist, an entrepreneur or a sales professional, your ability to gather good market information on your prospects or potential employers is essential. Begin by collecting the following data:

Name_____

Title_____

Company_____

Address_____

SIC code_____

Number of employees_____

Annual revenues_____

Key advisors (attorney, accountant, bank)
_____
_____

Organizational memberships (professional or social)
_____
_____

Committees _____
_____

Purchases (services and products they already have purchased)_____
_____

Seminars or tradeshows attended_____
_____

Publications read_____
_____

Any other unique information you can gather (what matters the most to them?)_____
_____
_____

Consider getting companies you buy from to sponsor an event with your local Chamber. As the coordinator, you will become the go-between for influential people, both in the Chamber, among the Chamber's membership base and with the companies you are working with or want to work with. You will be recognized as an influencer. People will come to you first when they want a person who has connections. You could create bigger and better connections and by the end of the year double your business.

Careerists

You are interested in making yourself known in your area of expertise. Set yourself up as a spokesperson about a particular concern in your industry. For instance, if you are in human resources, you might focus on such topics as "The Future of Employee Assistance Programs," or "What Effects Rightsizing or Downsizing Has Had in Today's Companies." By getting interviews with other companies who have been involved with these issues, you could become an industry expert. It will surprise you how your expert status in one area will help you build expert status in other areas. As you acquire leverage through this process, you can use one opportunity to open a door to another.

Sales Professionals

You want to acquire a number of customers, but your competition has dramatically increased and is eating up your new prospects. Get your company to host a party for your referral sources, as well as potential referral sources and prospects. Offer a roundtable (an interactive forum of no more than 30 people covering a topic of common interest). For example, you could present new products or ideas and get others to brainstorm on how you can use these products or services and why they are beneficial. Collaborate on establishing future roundtables, and invite your sources and their referred prospects. This project collaboration creates a steady stream of new referrals.

The Top Ten Networking Questions

Listed below are the ten networking questions I get asked most often and my responses to these questions:

1. *How do you locate the best networkers?*

   Ask, "Who do you know who is the best net-worker?" and "Why?" These two questions will help you locate people who are proactive networkers. The reason I added the question "Why?" was to make sure that your interpretation of what a good networker is would be similar to the person you have asked. You're looking for people who take the time to nurture others and build a mutual exchange. Once you locate these people through others, you can use the techniques and strategies outlined in this book to develop a MegaNetwork.

2. *Where are the best places to network?*

   The best places to network are wherever the best networkers are! Of course, if you are in a particular industry, you'll want to have a number of great networkers in that industry. Keep in mind, however, that a proactive networker in any industry will have better connections into your industry than an inactive networker within your industry. The way to experience the lowest risk and highest reward is to move from one good source to the next, asking, "What are the best organizations for me to join?"

3. *How do I initiate a conversation the first time I attend a networking gathering?*

This is a question I get asked again and again. Here are several strategies for maximizing your connections at any networking gathering:

- *Ask to be a guest.* As mentioned earlier, most organizations have something called a *New Membership Committee,* which is responsible for bringing in new members. Because there are so many organizations in existence today—with new ones springing up constantly—most have a rather high annual attrition rate. Organizations realize that in order to stay alive they constantly need to bring in new members. Many organizations don't have a formal plan for attracting and keeping new members. Help them out. By taking a proactive lead and asking to be the guest of someone on or in charge of the New Member Committee, you will help the group convince you to join their organization. Ask to be introduced to people. Because members of these committees are usually part of what I call an organization's Inner Circle, you will have the unique and powerful position of being new to an organization, but making strong connections up front.

  When you call, you might say, "Hi, I'm _____. I'm in sales with XYZ Company (or the owner of _____ currently looking for a position in this field). I'm interested in joining an organization such as yours. Would it be possible to be a guest of someone on your New Membership Committee or your board at your next gathering? Of course, I will pay my way."

- *Stand near the door.* This way you can introduce yourself to people who are just walking in. You might start the conversation by saying, "Hi, my name is Jerry Sanders. This is my first time here, how about you?" If the person knows people there, after you've told a little about yourself, you could ask, "Would you mind introducing me to someone you know? I'd love to meet some other new people." The best types of people to find in an organization are those who value their membership. They are more than happy to help you network to see if you would be interested in joining their organization.

  ◆ *If you are a member of an organization, sign up to be a greeter or registration assistant.*   Those seated at the registration table have a special opportunity to meet and greet people. Volunteer to be one of these people. You will be able to greet people as part of your responsibilities. If you talk with someone who makes you feel particularly comfortable, ask if you might sit with them. This is a good way of getting a broad view of networking possibilities.

4. *How do I break into a conversation where people are already talking?*

   If you find yourself in a situation where there are many small circles—some twos, some fours—yet no one standing alone, try this: Stand quietly but expressively next to a group that is open a bit. Try to stop yourself from feeling awkward with strong, positive self-talk, "It's okay. Soon someone will acknowledge me, and I will be able to introduce myself." Within a couple of minutes at the most, the group should recognize that they now have a new member and welcome you. If this doesn't happen, quietly move on. Realize that networkers today are much less cliquish. If you experience a group that is unusually aloof, this is the minority. These are not MegaNetworkers!

5. *How do I swap databases?*

    People are always looking for new contacts. One way to obtain them quickly is to ask someone for the names of people they know. When you get to a point in your networking where you have referral sources whom you trust, you can ask to swap databases. Understand that these names are more like leads than referrals. In other words, don't call these people saying that the other party referred you to them (unless this has been done). Use these names as a way to build larger bases of information. Those in my network often have similar contacts, but different relationships. The additional information you gather on these contacts will help you sell them on hiring you or buying your products or services faster.

    One networker who sold training programs swapped the base of contacts she had made over the past two years with mine. We both discovered new information about these contacts, such as what types of programs they had done in the past, what they said they were interested in doing in the future and who reported to whom, etc. This information helped us both develop a better awareness of our contacts' on-going and future needs, which helped us to tailor our respective marketing and sales efforts to meet those needs.

6. *What do I do when I feel uncomfortable in a situation?*

    First, DON'T BEAT YOURSELF UP! It is not your fault if you find yourself uncomfortable networking with a particular person or in a particular situation. I have found myself at gatherings where I just felt uncomfortable. I left and decided that for whatever reason, I was choosing to leave. This can happen to anyone. Get over it, and move on.

7. *What can I send to stay connected?*

Give something unique—everything from specialty cards and post cards (one great source for these is the Successories store) to uniquely designed letters (I send a letter on which I have printed a bright red plug that adds the words "Let's stay connected!" at the top.) There are also many ad specialty companies that have unique promotional gifts. I have seen everything from acrylic card holders with the recipient's business card placed inside to specialty baskets to stuffed animals.

- Give something that addresses the perceived or known interests of your source, prospect or hiring manager. Find out anything you can about the person you're sending something to that you know reflects one of their primary interests—golfing, sports, etc.

- Give something that connects your skills with your gift. I created a booklet that I sent out prior to publishing this book. *101 Ways to MegaNetwork, Giant Success Strategies for the '90s and Beyond* became the educational tool that I sent to stay connected. Many people who received the booklet ordered more for their colleagues and employees. The booklet showcased my skills in a nonthreatening way while simultaneously creating a promotional tool to generate further business opportunities.

Remember, creativity generates connections. You can use your creativity to generate interest in you and what you have to offer. If you can't come up with something creative, ask your friends. If your friends can't help you, try soliciting help from local marketing consultants who specialize in helping small businesses and individuals. An hour or two of professional time could help you get the start you need to move your networking into high gear—and, at a small price.

8. *How do I get the number of quality referrals that I need to build a MegaNetwork?*

   Focus! Remember, it's not *who* you know but *how* they know you. How people know you will come faster if they make a connection to you as someone special in a particular industry. We live in a society today that is "specialization focused." Don't limit your growth by trying to be too many things to too many markets. Your name will be on the tips of the tongues in your targeted industries much faster if you focus your networking to lead you to the influencers first. Once you connect with the influencers, either actively—through introductions—or passively—by having your name seen in publications or mentioned in the right places—you create leverage. This leverage helps you when you make contact. You will find your prospects saying, "Oh, I have heard or read about you."

   Second, participate. Get active in organizations. Participate in a committee for a special event. Rick Meyer, a very marketing-oriented accountant,was able to network with a number of proactive industry influencers when he joined his local Chamber and volunteered to help put on a series of special workshops for entrepreneurs. Rick's efforts helped generate new referral sources for both himself and the Chamber.

9. *How do I stay connected when I find that I don't have enough time to keep in touch with everyone?*

   Lack of time, a challenge second only to lack of confidence, can limit the success of your networking efforts. Remember the KISS Formula—KEEP

IT SIMPLE SWEETHEART. Prioritize. Stay connected through some of the simple techniques mentioned in the answer to question seven (above). Follow the 3-1-1 Rule created by young MegaNetworker, Rob Pioso: 3 days a week (try to stay with the same days) focus on spending even a half-hour a day reconnecting with existing contacts and sources or calling new ones; 1 day a week, a half-hour minimum, network internally with your fellow employees or colleagues; 1 day a week, a half-hour minimum, attend to the management of your contacts.

10. *How can I make sure that I am not too aggressive?*

Many networkers feel that they could be perceived as aggressive rather than assertive, which will result in repelling rather than attracting new opportunities. Assertive networkers, unlike aggressive networkers, respect the time and privacy of those with whom they seek to network. They constantly ask, "Is this a good time to call?" or "When would be a good time to contact you for a five-minute phone conversation?" Assertive networkers carry this respect to future exchanges. Their behavior is consistent, which builds trust. Assertive networkers earn the right to ask; they often receive things that others—who try to take without first giving—never get.

Total Quality Networking (TQN)

Creating the right connections is the key to MegaNetworking. As you have traveled through the process, I hope you have been able to see yourself making good use of the strategies and tactics presented.

The goal of MegaNetworking is to obtain the most powerful, positive, positioned, prolific connections—the 4 P's:

- *Powerful* people with the strongest influence
- *Positive* people who challenge you in positive, growth-oriented ways
- *Positioned* people who are poised for high growth
- *Prolific* people who can provide consistent, quality, continuous referrals

Final Tips

Stay in touch. Keep your sources informed of your progress with referrals and leads. This is true for the sources who refer job seekers, as well as sales professionals and entrepreneurs. Your sources gain when you gain. Periodic telephone calls or letters or cards keep your sources up-to-date—and validate their importance in your life.

In most cases, you should let your source know if something has not worked out. Look at the portion of the worksheet that says, "He Said, She Said" to give your source an overview of the conversation so that they can better help you build relationships with key prospects. This will help both of you assess future referrals.

Work from a position of influence to decision makers within companies. You have to hang in there day after day, month after month, year after year. Develop a system that works for you—today, tomorrow and always.

Know the characteristics of good referral sources. Revisit Chapter 4. Do your sources show you that they are interested through their actions? For example, do they lean toward you when they talk? Do they follow through on small commitments, such as calling back to give you a number?

You are looking for commitment from your referral sources that involves their actions more than just words. Susan RoAnne, keynote speaker and author of *How To Work a Room and the Secrets of Savvy Networking*, emphasizes that networking is primarily a right-brain function. She adds, "Some people are natural networkers. The problem is that networking is not a left-brain activity. Successful networking comes from the ability to do three things: 1) Communicate; 2) Make connections; and 3) Be vulnerable. You must especially have the courage to be vulnerable."

Make an affirmation of prosperity. Control your subconscious mind. Use visualization. Ask if everything went all right today and what you will have to do to improve. Refrain from dwelling on potential failures. Doubt and fear are a waste of time. Choose to ignore the negative. Choose to manage efficiently. Ask, "What can I do today?" and DO IT! Unlimit yourself. Tell yourself that you can't do it, have it or be a success unless you do:

Shine the spotlight on what is working. What did you do right? Let the positive feeling soak in. Absorb it. Look at the moment that is very successful, and focus on that. This is empowerment. In a world of gray matter, say NO to some things. Set some boundaries, which will help you get to the Yes faster. SIMPLIFY. What can you throw away?

Rate yourself today in different areas. Give yourself a slightly higher rating in your strengths, then stretch to achieve it. If you have a vision, it's more real than anything you know and it's the most powerful thing.

Grow your confidence. Move from hope to confidence to trust to knowing that you can accomplish what you set out to achieve. Focus on the person in networking, not the project. Develop active listening skills.

Maintain relationships. Relationship maintenance is vital to building a MegaNetwork. Keep contacts alive by making a new connection each time you speak. Avoid merely continuing the old. Keep thinking laterally of different things that the person you are talking to could do or different people they could connect with to improve their connections.

Give something. Bring your talent. You might not always be able to reciprocate through leads or referrals, but more likely than not you have some strengths where your sources do not. For example, I offer to help my sources by reading over anything they have written. What do your sources need help doing? Perhaps you can be of help.

Get feedback. Solicit your sources' suggestions for improving your results. Ask for three suggestions. Be specific about what you are seeking. "Who do you know who can use these skills?"

Don't let life just happen to you. Happen to life. Create the kind of world that you want to live in and others will line up behind you.

Through your commitment to a Total Quality Network, you will realize the rewards of the MegaNetworking System within a very short time. You will be able to take advantage of your network for a lifetime, getting twice the results in half the time. Whenever you find yourself lapsing into a general *meeting and greeting* process of building relationships, realize that the quality will quickly disappear (as will the number of referrals) if you don't MegaNetwork.

Just as with any lifetime reward, successful networking takes time and effort up front. But the snowball effect is amazing. Through their persistence, those who took the time to cultivate their MegaNetworks now reap the rewards of their years of preparation and implementation—just as a big snowball rolls down a hill, gathering speed and snow as it moves. There will be times when opportunities may be lean, but you will always be able to return to your sources for support and assistance. With your MegaNetwork, the journey is the reward. Remember most of all to enjoy the ride.

 # Use Your Network To Help You

A strategy for avoiding networking purgatory is to watch for *energy vampires*. Energy vampires are people who continually ask but seldom give. Each time you meet them, they drain small amounts of your energy. These people leave you feeling physically drained. Replace them with proactive people who appreciate you.

You will recognize energy vampires by the requests that they make. They want more time than you really have to give, and they want a lot of it often. The way to prevent energy vampires from taking over your time is to schedule those times when you will take or make calls and network. Your commitment to keeping some type of structure and your consistency regarding that structure will be the only tools you will have to make certain that you will not allow others to take advantage of you.

- *Make a difference in your own life first.* If you first make a difference in your own life, then you can make a difference in the lives of others. Steven Covey talks about the habits of highly effective people and places an emphasis on personal effectiveness. You must be personally effective before you can be interpersonally effective.

- *Keep a sense of humor.* Find people who have a keen sense of humor. A sense of humor will decrease the stress that can build up and make you less effective in your relationships. Therefore, a sense of humor helps you take your work less seriously, allows enjoyment to build excitement and provides you with a greater challenge.

- *Be prepared.*   Not being prepared is like catching a ball without a catcher's mitt. As a child, I enjoyed playing softball regularly. Every now and then, I invited another friend to play who did not have a catcher's mitt. When I lent my mitt to my friend, he became more prepared, but then I was less prepared. Make sure that you put on your catcher's mitt before going out to network. Take plenty of business cards with you and small tablets to jot down notes. Set goals for yourself each week concerning the amount of time you will set aside for networking and the number of people that you will contact.

- *Stay connected.*   Put your connection time in perspective. One MegaNetworker reports that 20 to 30 minutes a week comes out to only 25 hours (or approximately one day) annually with each referral source. If you have ten referral sources—which is really all you need—ten days a year is not a great deal of time to spend in developing relationships that will last a lifetime.

- *Think about different ways to network.*   Industry or association meetings, trade group meetings, trade shows, social functions, etc. are great ways to network. Each one will require a different form of networking and require you to change your networking process slightly. Some networking opportunities will be more formal and some less formal. Always attend with the strategy of being an *information gatherer* rather than a *business pusher*. The time to do most of your exchanging will come later.

- *Know what your no's are.*   Know the difference between selfish and self-caring. Caring about yourself is quite different from being selfish. Sometimes, it's just better to say "no," when you're overworked.

You, your clients and your network will be better off because of it. And doing something for yourself isn't selfish A walk, a concert, a movie or a trip to the gym are activities that will revitalize you.

- *Incorporate these four P's:*   Plan (written rehearsal), Prepare (visual rehearsal), Practice (verbal rehearsal) and Perform (physical rehearsal). Plan by creating a written rehearsal of what you wish to achieve. You are gaining optimum skills. Prepare by practicing a visual rehearsal of seeing yourself in a relaxed state with a group of people, one person at a time, exchanging information or sharing/gathering information. Practice by verbally role playing, in advance, the things you might say to new contacts. Perform by asking friends and referral sources to role play with you.

- *Keep modeling successful networkers.*   Look for successful networkers; ask others to identify successful networkers, meet with these successful networkers to discover what they do to build their networks and then model them.

- *Adhere to networking etiquette.*   I talked about networking etiquette before, and I can't say enough about developing a level of etiquette and common courtesy for others. It's a small world, and you will find that your courtesy will be greatly appreciated and precede you as a courteous networker.

- *Take responsibility.*   Taking responsibility means actually responding to the ability that you have within you to perform certain actions.

In this *age of responsibility*—look to yourself first and then to others to co-create opportunities.

Staying
Connected

Throughout *Make Your Connections Count*, I have tried to address the needs of anyone interested in creating new business opportunities or landing a new job. I have seen dramatic results achieved by people who have implemented the MegaNetworking System and its strategies. Obviously no one strategy will ensure success, but certain strategies are much more effective than others.

What I like most about the MegaNetworking System is that anyone can use it. It is a system that becomes more useful over time. There are several sayings that have particular relevance to MegaNetworking. One is, "It's lonely at the top." That's how it might be for most, but for MegaNetworkers, the top is the place where all the fun happens. One of my greatest dreams is to travel around the world and visit all the people I have helped. I imagine myself walking into restaurants especially, where people whisper, "Do you know who that is?" The owners run up to greet me and introduce me to their best customers. Of course, dinner is on them, and in turn, I get to share all their pride in their success!

Another traditional saying goes something like, "It gets harder the higher up the ladder you get." Well, it's just the reverse with MegaNetworking. Here, you find people who are connected with others like themselves. As you build your MegaNetwork, you educate your sources and they educate you on how to benefit each other. Ultimately, you set up a continuous stream of introductions that result in more and more opportunities.

Throughout the MegaNetworking process, I have focused on an alliance of style, strategy and substance. I went beyond *how* to network effectively, to *where* (organizations, networking groups) and *with whom* (industry influencers, referral sources, etc.). Ultimately, MegaNetworking moves toward building cooperative opportunities to work together in teams on a project by project basis.

Support and alliances are truly easier to realize today than they've ever been. As the result of re-engineering at so many companies, more and more talented people are saying, "I'm going to operate on my own, now. But, I would prefer to partner with people in an effort to achieve the goals that I now have established for myself." Through this ongoing awareness of partnering opportunities with independents, freelancers, consultants and executives, there is unlimited potential to build a network that is much stronger than we could have built within a traditional corporate setting.

Because there is so much more understanding of the value of connecting today, you now have a greater opportunity than ever before to build powerful, exciting associations that carry you beyond traditional business relationships into lifetime friendships. No longer are corporations dedicated to taking care of you for life. You have more responsibility in the '90s. You have the *opportunity* to grow through thoughtful, challenging and rewarding relationships.

We are all people with skills who will be brought into corporations for *projects* rather than long-term *jobs*. We will work in teams with many other independents as we are outsourced by large corporations. This offers opportunities to the careerist, the entrepreneur and the sales professional.

In this dynamic, changing workplace, we can either view the glass as half-empty or half-full. We must begin to understand that we are not in this alone. We are at a point in our historical growth when our relationships can make the difference between incredible success or isolation and misery. We have changed our choices. There are choices now that anyone can make and build quickly into opportunities. The choices are ours. The opportunities are ours. All we have to do is seize the day!

Let's Stay Connected!

For further information on my interactive seminars, speeches and coaching, or for comments, questions or compliments, please contact me at:

Practice Development Institute (PDI)/FERS Group
401 North Michigan Avenue, 26th Floor
Chicago, IL 60611-4240
Fax: (708) 310-8386

If you would be interested in receiving a free sample of my quarterly *MegaLetter*, please provide your name, company name (if applicable), address, phone and fax numbers when you fax.

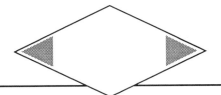

Appendix I:

Special Tips for
Sales Professionals and
Entrepreneurs

Strategies for Prospecting

If you are responsible for generating sales, then networking becomes your optimum tool. One of the best networking strategies you can create is that of *cross-selling* or opening doors for others—your referral sources—and having them open doors for you. When you are on a sales call, either internally or externally, give your business to people who have given to you or have the potential to give to you. This is the best opportunity for obtaining new business through others. Also, when you look at people who have the opportunity, don't forget to look for people who are reciprocators, so that you can see that return referral coming quickly and rather effortlessly.

The way to open doors for others is to MegaNetwork. For example, when you're on a sales call, mention members of your network who would do a good job for your prospect. Be an active resource for others.

This shows that you are committed to a longer term relationship and that your focus is on the continuous co-creation of opportunities for those with whom you do business.

It is not what you know, it's who knows you. Do your prospects know you? Do your prospects know others who know you? Do your prospects know your product or service? If the answer to these questions is "No," why should your prospects use you? However, if you can turn these no's into yeses through introductions and information given by your sources, you have a much better chance of finding new clients, customers or jobs.

How do you do that? First, get through to the people who know the decision maker or can refer you to others. Then build relationships with these people so that they have favorable impressions of you. Many businesses make group decisions or at least ask for impressions from others whom they know. Therefore, the more people who know you either directly or indirectly and think favorably of you, the better chance you have of obtaining any new business opportunities you seek. Another way to build consensus is to repeat what another has said. This clarifies and builds awareness of agreement.

Use objections as fuel, not as bullets. Objections should be used as a fuel to build a better awareness and a buy-in to whatever you are looking to sell.

Calling a Prospect—How To Deliver an Effective Introduction

Just as a headline is the most important part of an advertisement, your introduction is the most important

part of the networking exchange. Therefore make the first words out of your mouth add to your appearance and behavior. Your introduction should hook your listeners, making them want more information. Give them as little as possible, however, turning the conversation to them as quickly as possible.
  Example:

JJ: "Hi, my name is John Jones, what's yours?"

SS: "Sue Smith."

JJ: "Nice to meet you Sue. What do you do?"

SS: "I own a video store. What do you do John?"

JJ: "I'm the best friend of the entrepreneur."

SS: "Really, what do you mean by that?"

JJ: "I help entrepreneurs spend as little as possible for the greatest return. For example, I might help a retail store like yours create a plan that would enable you either to sell your business for a good price when you were ready or to open new stores."

SS: "That sounds very interesting. Tell me more."

(Now turn the conversation toward your potential contact. Start asking questions)

JJ: "Well, how long have you been in business?"

SS: "My husband and I bought this store last year."

JJ: "How are things going?"

SS: "Oh, all right. Of course, we would like to be making more money."

JJ: "Our accounting firm offers a free second opinion on taxes; we also have small business roundtables focused on your industry. Perhaps you would like to attend one as our guest?"

(Your goal is to lay the foundation for a relationship of trust and respect. You are building a relationship whether you can help this person now or sometime in the future. You haven't given away any secrets, you have just alerted your contact to the fact that they may have needs that they hadn't recognized before—needs that, sooner or later, should be addressed.)

Listening for Needs

Good listening skills are crucial to revealing needs that can be met by your services or products. Below is an example of a conversation that might be developed with a prospect.

You:	"Steve, you mentioned that you've owned your company for five years now. How has business been lately?" (open-ended question).
Steve:	"Well, I think the economy is getting better. We're looking at some new projects."
You:	"That's great. Can you tell me about one of them?"
Steve:	"Sure, one of them is working with the government. We haven't done much business with the government, though."
You:	"Really, perhaps I can be of some assistance. We have someone at our firm who has helped clients work with the government."
Steve:	"I would appreciate that."
You:	"Why don't I call you tomorrow, and we can arrange a time to get together to find out more about your business."
Steve:	"That would be fine."

A Strategy for Getting Prospects To Bond with You

As mentioned before, one very effective bonding strategy is to repeat, from time to time, in the other person's words or in yours, what you think they just said. These words create building blocks of agreement that help you grow a long-lasting relationship. I find that by repeating peoples' thoughts back to them in a slightly different way, I help bond the relationship because the other party is pleased that I understand their need. I also help them see things in a different perspective.

For example:

Mark: "As I was saying, I'm finding it very difficult to uncover marketing methods that work for me. I have tried public relations, direct mail and telemarketing over the past five years, but nothing brings in the returns that I want. Often I don't even recoup the dollars I put into the efforts.

M.G.: "I understand. You would love to develop a marketing mix that would really show some profit."

Mark: "Exactly, but I don't know how to do that."

M.G.: "Have you found that one method is better than another?"

Mark: "Yes, it seems that our telemarketing was going well for a while. We were getting appointments pretty steadily, but not as many as we needed to keep myself and my two other employees active."

M.G.: "What list were you using?"

Mark: "We just used names from a directory of service companies in the area."

M.G.:	"Were there any particular types of service businesses where you found it easy to make appointments?"
Mark:	"Why, yes. We did seem to have better luck with insurance agencies and banks than any other type of business."
M.G.:	"Have you analyzed why that might be the case?"
Mark:	"Not really. We really didn't know what to do with that information. We want to build this company, but we are obviously doing something wrong."
M.G.:	"Have you considered creating a plan that will identify profitable marketing and sales strategies that will help you increase your profits?"
Mark:	"That sounds great. How do we do that?"
M.G.:	"Well, the next step would be to sit down and put down on paper what you have already done. I am available in the morning next Wednesday and in the afternoon next Thursday. Which would be better for you?"

Key Account Strategies

Prior to establishing her own sales training firm, Pat David sold consulting services for a Chicago-based telecommunications firm. Pat overcame nearly impossible odds to win a telecommunications consulting contract for a Fortune 500 company, which we will call ABC Company. This story and the mind map on the following page depict a real-life example of the advantages of networking with an outside influencer (inside coach).

Pat learned through a networking contact that ABC Company (see the Mind Map in Figure A1.1) planned to build a new world headquarters facility. It would be looking for a new telecommunications system for the facility through a Request for Proposal (RFP). When Pat called the company to inquire about the RFP, she learned that proposals would be solicited from approximately 26 other consulting firms of various backgrounds. "The least attractive role to play in the sales environment is that of the proverbial *needle in the haystack*," Pat advises. Without a well thought out strategy, you would end up as just another unknown bidder in the sales process. When Pat received the RFP, her concerns grew.

The RFP was only five pages long and described the project needs in dangerously general terms. Considering that this was a world headquarters relocation, the RFP's brevity was risky for both ABC Company and any firm wishing to respond with a proposal. The greatest danger was the absence of detail for critical project requirements and a very broad description of the project's scope.

As a result, most firms responding would be inclined to underestimate the cost for conducting this major project. This would most likely result in cost overruns as details of the project unfolded. In addition to potential overruns, any firm choosing to allow for such broad uncertainties might, in fact, overestimate their cost and ultimately price themselves out of contention for the business. In addition to these challenges, the RFP was received on December 15. Responses were due on January 1. Even without the holidays, ABC Company had not allowed enough time for vendors to prepare a legitimate response.

Fortunately Pat learned through her original networking source that a general consultant had already been hired by ABC Company's controller to oversee the entire world headquarters building project. His responsibilities also included the management of all other outside consultants working on the job. Pat called the general consultant and found him to be very receptive. He was well aware of the significance of the project and of the potential negative impact that unsatisfactory telecommunications services in the new facility could have upon the entire relocation project. Through him, Pat also learned that the individuals (who already had a favorite vendor) conducting the telecommunications consulting process were not the actual decision makers. They would simply make the recommendations to ABC Company's controller. Pat also was able to determine that the controller would be totally inaccessible to all prospective proposers. Pat had to sell to the RFP authors who would, in turn, make the recommendation to the controller who was driving the decision behind the scene.

Pat's goals for responding to the RFP became clear. First, she had to respond by the requested date to even be considered for the project. She decided that she would use the RFP's brevity and the project's uncertainties to her advantage. Pat decided to respond with an offer of three different fee packages (low, middle and high), and to state in her proposal that she needed additional information in order to narrow cost ranges.

Pat's proposal would not only provide pricing, it would also need to tactfully identify and raise serious questions regarding areas not addressed in the abbreviated RFP. With this strategy Pat would be able to respond in a timely manner and achieve her most important goals. Pat needed more time and information to develop a more realistic approach to a world headquarters relocation. She had to arrange for a face-to-face meeting with the authors of the RFP. Above all, Pat had to somehow enhance her position with the authors while indirectly attracting the attention of the controller. She needed to increase her visibility.

Pat shared her concerns and her strategy with the general consultant. She knew that if she could make him aware of the risks already present in the project, he would likely bring them to the attention of the controller.

Pat's unusual proposal was submitted on time and received the desired results. She was granted a face-to-face meeting to discuss details of the relocation project with the RFP's authors. Ultimately Pat was provided important information and a lot of additional time to develop a comprehensive project strategy.

At every critical juncture in the sales process, Pat contacted the general consultant for feedback and gave him the opportunity to funnel critical issues back to the controller. At all times, Pat continued to remain alert to any news from other networking contacts regarding the project in general and other related developments. With the help and direction provided by her sales network, Pat was able to speak to the concerns of the authors and outside influencers, as well as those of the controller. Pat tailored discussions with the influencers to address their concerns, while supplying written documentation in her proposal that would ultimately be provided to the controller directly addressing his requirements. Although, Pat never met or spoke directly with the controller, she was successful in winning an exciting consulting project.

Figure A1.1 is a Mind Map designed by Pat that demonstrates how she moved through the initial stages of the MegaNetworking process to obtain connections with key influencers to the decisionmaker.

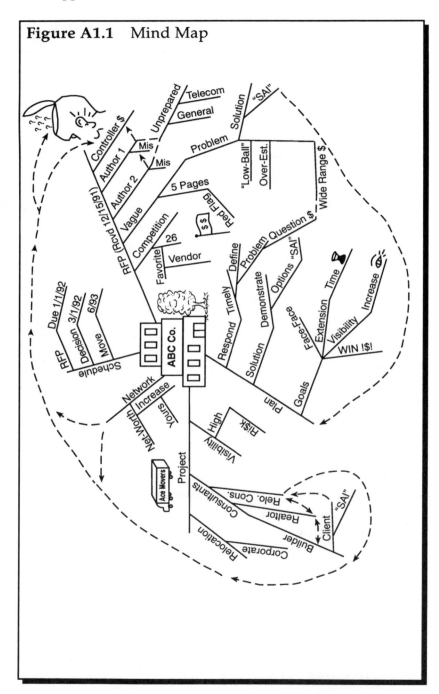

Figure A1.1   Mind Map

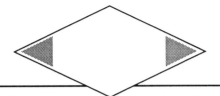

Appendix II:

Special Tips for
Job Seekers and Careerists

If you are a careerist, you are constantly looking for the best job—the job that offers the best working conditions, best opportunities to sharpen your skills and of course, the best pay. By first finding those people you would most like to work with, you will accelerate the job hunting process. Always ask those you network with the names of anyone they know or hear about firsthand who would be great to work with. If you have easy access to that person, take the time to get to know him or her. The more of these people you know ahead of time, the easier it will be to get into a new job if your old one should suddenly become extinct! Here are two success stories to help you gain more insight into the MegaNetworking process for job seekers and careerists:

Phillip Jimenez is a MegaNetworker. He knew that the odds were not in his favor to land the job he really wanted in today's competitive job market. Yet, Phil did get a great job, in less than three months, at a salary that was $10,000 more than he had expected! How did he do it?

Phil followed the steps to creating a MegaNetwork. His first base of contacts involved prospective employers at a local job fair. Although the representatives at the fair were not encouraging to Phil, he still took the time to build rapport with them. You see, Phil didn't go to the fair focusing on getting a particular job; he went to learn the needs of employers in various industries.

Even more interesting, the Fortune 500 company that ended up hiring Phil had a representative at the show who was particularly discouraging. She told Phil all the reasons why it would be almost impossible for him to get a job at her company—their market was not growing as quickly as they had anticipated, they were losing market share to foreign competitors, they were not even sure that they could guarantee if they gave him a job that his job category would still be in existence in four years!

Phil left the fair feeling discouraged but happy that he had focused on the needs of the companies he met rather than his own. This way he was able to gather a wealth of information to take back and reflect on how his current skills fit the job he wanted.

When Phil did get a call from the Fortune 500 company mentioned above, he was actually hesitant to take the job. He asked, "How can you guarantee that my job will be around in four years?" The recruiter assured Phil that they would support him in making a task change to a new job that was more suited to the company's changing needs.

The initiative Phil followed—to remain open to all possibilities (withholding judgment) and staying in contact with the prospective employer—dramatically increased his chances of getting a position. Phil was able to look beyond the immediate opportunity to get a job. He got to know the person he was speaking with the day of the job fair and continued through her to exchange information as to how his skills would be beneficial to the company today and in the future. What Phil learned through his job search can now be carried into the company to build internal alliances.

Amy Brand used similar strategies to acquire a job in the field of computer training. She happened to be in an elevator when two human resource administrators were discussing the need to hire two more trainers. Amy, who had a degree in computers, had been looking for a job for some time. She had been working as a temporary when she encountered the administrators. Having her resume handy in her briefcase, Amy didn't hesitate to take the initiative, pull the resume out and hand it to one of the men. "Would you mind considering me for the position?" she asked. The two men smiled at her, took the resume and left.

Of course, Amy had no idea if anything further would happen, but she decided to take advantage of the opportunity placed in her path. As many leaders have stated, "Success happens when preparation meets opportunity." When the call came the next day for an interview, Amy happily walked the two flights up from where she had been temping. She was told as the two men offered her the position how pleased they were to see someone with such strong initiative.

Both Phil and Amy are new to networking. Yet, because they are aware of the choice they have—between a baseline network and a MegaNetwork—they can now grow their relationships proactively. Phil and Amy have futures that hold great potential through the shared efforts of everyone in their separate networks. With their network, they can create the job that would be best suited to their skills and interests. It may not happen with their first job, but Phil and Amy will get better and better at educating their network and eventually will create just what they want. Like Amy or Phil, you now have the strategy to build a lifetime network of proactive participants. It requires just the effort on your part and the willingness to STAY CONNECTED!

The following career networking suggestions are excerpted from *Getting Hired in the '90s* by Vicki L. Spina, published by Corporate Image Publishers. The book is available to order by calling (800) 247-6553.

Where To Look for a New Position

Business and networking contacts are extremely important in uncovering hidden career opportunities. Tell everyone you know and meet that you are active in the job market. When individuals are unemployed, they have a tendency to hide from the business world. Encourage yourself to stay active and communicate with past business contacts and friends. The ideal position will not come knocking on your door—you need to go out and find it. Design and print a personal business card with your name and phone number and desired position and pass it out to everyone you know and meet. (Optional: Print a 20-30 word statement about your uniqueness on the back.)

Start networking by making a list of everyone you know:

> Business Acquaintances, Business Associates, Coworkers (be discreet)
>
> Church or Synagogue Members
>
> Clients*
>
> Doctors, Dentists and Lawyers

---

*Note: I usually do not advocate telling clients. However, if you have an unusually close relationship, they may be a good source of contacts.

Figure A2.1 Networking Pie

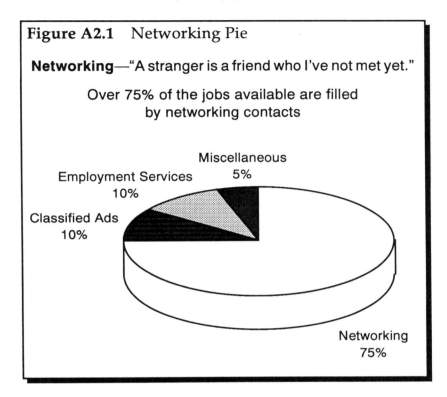

Networking—"A stranger is a friend who I've not met yet."

Over 75% of the jobs available are filled by networking contacts

Miscellaneous 5%

Employment Services 10%

Classified Ads 10%

Networking 75%

Ex-Bossses and Past Co-Workers

Former Professors, Teachers, Students

Friends and Health Club Members

In addition to networking, there are several other means to uncovering job openings. Listed below are 15 lead generators.

1. Alumni Associations (check with your college for detailed information)
2. Association Meetings (select associations related to your chosen industry through the *Encyclopedia of Associations*)
3. Classified Advertisements
4. College Placement Offices (even if you did not attend their school)

5. Conventions

6. Database Services (Résumé On Computer, etc.)

7. Employment Agencies

8. Job Fairs (check with your local newspapers and Chamber of Commerce for upcoming events)

9. Job Support Groups (often held at local libraries, chuches, synagogues)

10. Local Networking Groups (many networking groups announce their meeting dates in local newspapers. Or check you local Chamber of Commerce for upcoming events)

11. Local Unemployment Office

12. On-Line Networks: Prodigy, Internet, Online Career Center, etc. (must have computer modem)*

13. Research Contacts (contacts you've uncovered from the newspapr, trade and business magazines, etc.)

14. Seminars (attend workshops related to your industry)

15. Temporary Agencies/Contract Firms

Next, develop a 20-30 word statement that describes what is unique about you

Key Qualities of a Successful Job Seeker

1. *Attitude*   Enthusiastic, happy and confident.

2. *Image*   Displays a professional appearance at all times.

3. *Prepared*   Researches company before the interview. Plans and practices answers in advance.

---

*Note: For additional information on high-tech solutions to job hunting, read *Electronic Job Search Revolution,* by Joyce Lain Kennedy and Thomas Morrow (John Wiley & Sons, $12.95)

4. *Action* Spends majority of day developing leads and interviews, stays actively involved in job search—doesn't hide out.

5. *Rapport* Friendly and likable, the interviewer is glad to have you there—you make them feel good.

6. *Presentation* Is able to describe themselves in a manner that excites the employer and convinces him or her to make an offer. Uses a Feature/Benefit Presentation to get hired.

7. *Closes* Summarizes the interview by re-emphasizing strengths and by asking for the job.

8. *Follow-up* Timely and pleasant follow-up (creatively) to reiterate interest, desire and ability to handle the job.

9. *Tenacity* Doesn't give up, handles rejections well—keeps forging ahead, knowing that a better opportunity is just around the corner. Doesn't take rejections personally.

Comparison of Key Qualities of Successful Job Seeker to Salesperson

1. *Attitude* Projects confidence in self and his/her product or service.

2. *Image* Makes a good first impression. Appearance reflects success and professionalism.

3. *Prepared* Researches clients needs and tailor makes a presentation outlining how he/she can fulfill those needs.

4. *Action* 100 Percent COMMITMENT to developing leads—doesn't wait for clients to call—*actively pursues new opportunities by networking, involvement in industry activities and cold calling.* Spends majority of day generating new business.

5. *Rapport*   Establishes a sincere relationship with client—client enjoys speaking with salesperson.

6. *Presentation*   Describes service or product using a FEATURE/BENEFIT presentation that meets the needs of the client.

7. *Closes*   Summarizes the sales call by asking for the order and overcomes any concerns or objections client may have.

8. *Follow-up*   Persistent about staying in touch with client without getting defensive or angry. Doesn't let a NO or rejection get in his/her way.

9. *Tenacity*   Understands that he/she needs to hear some NOs before he/she gets a YES. When rejections occur he/she critiques his/her presentation, learns what he/she can do better the next time then takes the necessary action.

In addition to the opportunities listed above, it is imperative that you make a list of every single person you know. Give them a copy of your résumé (perhaps for internal positions posted in their company) as well as openings they may hear about elsewhere.

Other great sources for networking include:

Members of health clubs, churches or synagogues, doctors, lawyers, support groups, trade or industry associations, and don't forget ex-employers, teachers or former co-workers. If you are currently employed and seeking a career change, be discreet when networking. Word travels fast and could reach your current employer quickly.

Now that you know where the jobs are, it's up to you. Get prepared, take action and you will be on your way to a successful new career.

Note: Read the 1994 edition of *The Professional's Job Finder* for tremendous networking opportunities.

Making Phone Calls   What day or days and hours of the week will you make your networking calls? Write these days and times down to help you allocate time for becoming a proactive networker.

Day(s)	*Time(s)*
_____	_____
_____	_____
_____	_____
_____	_____
_____	_____
_____	_____

Suggestions

* Schedule calls with networking sources just as you would a face-to-face meeting. Put the letter "P" beside your name to note that this is a phone meeting. Use the Referral Source Meeting Summary and accompanying call documents to keep your calls focused.

* Handle return calls for first-time networking by setting up a good time each day when you can take return calls and try to keep to that time of day. Cluster your calls together.

* State your purpose for calling up front (For example "John, I'm calling to see if we might get together to see if we can exchange business leads and referrals with each other?" or "Sally, I got your name from George."

Appendix III:

Your Networking Plan

Why Plan?

The average person wastes three days out of every month looking for things. Keep these pages at your fingertips, so that they can be found easily. Also, noting the time you take to plan will pay off ten-fold in results. You will be more organized and confident.

Your Vision

Your vision is the *big picture* of what you want to accomplish over the long term, say five years from now. (For example, a careerist may want to become president of a company. An entrepreneur may want to franchise his or her business. A sales professional may want to become manager of a sales team.) What is *your* vision?

_____

_____

Your Mission Statement

A mission statement is your personal statement of purpose. Why are you here? You should have a personal mission as well as a company mission (if you are in the position, i.e. own a company). Your mission statement will serve as the foundation for your growth. My mission is to help others create and maintain interpersonal effectiveness through one-on-one coaching, speaking and writing. What's your mission?

_____

_____

Goal Setting

Write down your networking goals:

I. Short Range (One Month)   Date ___/___/___

_____

II. Mid Range (3 Months)   Date ___/___/___

_____

III. Long Range (1 year)   Date ___/___/___

_____

Making Phone Calls

What day or days and hours of the week will you make your networking calls? Write these days and times down to help you allocate time for becoming a proactive networker.

Day(s)   *Time(s)*

_____   _____

_____   _____

_____   _____

_____   _____

Suggestions

- Schedule calls with networking sources just as you would a face-to-face meeting. Put the letter P beside your source's name to note that this is a phone meeting. Use the Referral Source Worksheet and accompanying call documents to keep your calls focused.

- Handle return calls for first-time networking by setting up a good time each day when you can take return calls and try to keep to that time of day. Cluster your calls together.

- State your purpose for calling up front. (For example: "John, I'm calling to see if we might get together to exchange business leads and referrals with each other," or "Sally, I got your name from George. George told me that in your line of work you often refer accountants. Could we set up a meeting to discuss how we might help one another in our respective businesses?")

Objectives

Objectives are even more definable than goals. Use the SMART formula (S = specific, m = measureable, a = attainable, r = realistic and t = tangible) to help you achieve your goals:

State two or three objectives for networking in the next month:

1. Number of contacts you will make in the next month _____ three months _____ six months _____ year _____
2. Number of referral sources you will have within the next month _____ three months _____ six months _____ year _____
3. Number of referral source meetings you will have within the next month _____ three months _____ six months _____ year _____
4. Number of new leads or referrals you will work with your referral sources to help you obtain with the next month _____ three months _____ six months _____ year _____

Strategies

Strategies are basic routes that you will take to achieve your objectives. Later, you will describe detailed plans for implementing strategies. Strategies may relate to more than one objective. Write down the strategies that you will use to accomplish the objectives listed above. For example, a strategy you might use for getting new contacts will be to attend certain association meetings within the next month or call certain people you currently know who can help you locate new contacts.

1. Strategies for reaching previously described objective #1:

_____

_____

2. Strategies for reaching previously described objective #2:

_____

_____

3. Strategies for reaching previously described objective #3:

_____

_____

4. Strategies for reaching previously described objective #4

_____

_____

Uniqueness

Describe what is unique about you or your company (services or products) and how you meet an unfilled need in your target market. What are the benefits you offer? This is your competitive edge in your target market.

_____

_____

Market Overview and Size

How big is your target market? (For example, if it is local, there may be 200 companies; if you have a national market, it will be much larger) Look for markets that are expanding rather than shrinking.

_____

_____

Brief overview and history of your target market

_____

_____

_____

Prospect Profile

Why will your prospect buy from you? Describe . . .

- Type of person (owner, manager, purchasing agent, etc.)
- Demographics & sociographics (age, income, occupation)
- Pychographics (Motivations)—(Prestige, fear, peer pressure)

Types of prospects and why you chose to target them

_____

_____

_____

_____

_____

_____

Who are your best prospects? List the top ten companies that you want to sell to or work for:

1. _____

2. _____

3. _____

4. _____

5. _____

6. _____

7. _____

8. _____

9. _____

10. _____

Competition

Assess your competition. List major competitors, their market share, strategies, marketing methods and financial conditions.

1. Major competitors and dollar volume or percent of market

_____

_____

_____

_____

2. Strengths and weaknesses of competitors

_____

_____

_____

_____

3. Strategy and marketing methods (current and anticipated)

_____

_____

_____

_____

4. Financial condition

_____

_____

_____

_____

Market Share

How do you currently rank in your market compared to your competitors? (1 being very noncompetitive and 5 being very competitive).

1. Where your business ranks versus competitors in the market _____
2. Market share data

Competitor (Name)   Estimated Share

_____   _____

_____   _____

_____   _____

_____   _____

Geographic Market Factors

Where are your prime prospects?

_____

_____

_____

Dynamic Positioning Strategies

Marketing strategies are your route to success. We are focusing on the most effective marketing strategy to-day—networking. Use your knowledge of:

- The industry
- Market niche
- Customers
- Competition
- Your uniqueness

as the foundation of your strategies. Outline the methods that will result in more sales or a new job.

How are you going to:

• identify target contacts?

_____

_____

_____

• identify target lead/referral sources?

_____

_____

_____

• identify industry influencers?

_____

_____

_____

• identify associations where you will network?

_____

_____

_____

_____

• identify other locations to network (e.g. church, social gatherings, volunteer organizations)?

_____

_____

_____

_____

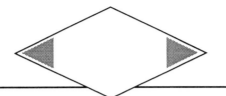

Appendix IV:

Resources and References

Figure A4.1 Referral Source Meeting Summary

Lead/Referral (circle) **Source** (list)

Name/Title_____

Company Name_____

Address_____

City/State/Zip_____

Telephone_____

Meeting Information

Today's date/time_____

Last meeting date/time_____

Next meeting date/time_____

Section I - Referral Log of Names

Name	Telephone	Address	Rank

Section II - Project Collaborations

_____
_____
_____
_____
_____

Section III - To Do (prioritize)

1._____
2._____
3._____
4._____
5._____

Section IV - (a) Who do you know? or (b) Do you know?

_____
_____
_____
_____
_____

Figure A4.2   Prospect Data Sheet

Lead/Referral (circle)   **Source** (list)

Name_____

Title_____

Company Name_____

Address_____

City/State/Zip_____

Telephone_____

S.I.C. Code/Type of Business_____

Additional Information

Reads What Publications_____

Values_____

Interests_____

Club Affiliations_____

Other_____

_____

Date	I Said	He/She Said
_____	_____	_____
_____	_____	_____
_____	_____	_____
_____	_____	_____
_____	_____	_____
_____	_____	_____
_____	_____	_____

Figure A4.3 Correspondence Log

L=Lead R=Referral	Name/Company	Telephone	Address	Result

Figure A4.4   Referral Source Meeting Summary

Lead/Referral (circle)   **Source** (list)
Name/Title _John Smith - President_
Company Name _RJ Company_
Address _422 E. Drake_
City/State/Zip _Milwaukee, Wisconsin_
Telephone _342-5256_

Meeting Information
Today's date/time _9/10_
Last meeting date/time _9/1 - phone_
Next meeting date/time _9/20_

Section I - Referral Log of Names

Name	Telephone	Address	Rank
Sally Connor	362-9110	420 LandsFair - RM	Might need
			Benefits
Greg Frakes	525-1005	895 Cambrige - SCH	Cafeteria Plan

Section II - Project Collaborations

Possible joint seminar for clients and prospects
focusing on compensation plans.

Section III - To Do (prioritize)

1. _Call Great Lakes Chamber - Possible speaking_
2. _engagement (708) 321-8521_
3. _Call Janet for John - Might know a good lawyer_
4.
5.

Section IV - (a) Who do you know? or (b) Do you know?

A) _Anyone in State Chamber? - Steve Mandalla_
_(708) 771-3621_
B) _June Abrahms - Executive Director -_
Park Ridge Chamber

Figure A4.5   Prospect Data Sheet

Lead/Referral (circle)   **Source** (list)

Name _Sally Connor_

Title _President_

Company Name _ABC Company_

Address _420 LandsFair_

City/State/Zip _Milwaukee, Wisconsin_

Telephone _(708) 362-9110_

S.I.C. Code/Type of Business _Temporary Services_

Additional Information

Reads What Publications _Modern Office, Exec. Secretary_

Values _Integrity, Fairness_

Interests _Skiing, Roller Blading_

Club Affiliations _National Association for Temp Services_

Other _Wants to learn how to golf._

Date	"I Said"	"He/She Said"
5/10	Hi, Sally, my name is Anne Berm. John Smith gave me your name and said you might be interested in looking at purchasing a benefits package for your employees.	Yes. Thanks for calling. John told me about your firm. I really don't know what kind of benefits I should offer my employees.
	Why don't we set an appointment for next week and I'll go over all your options.	Great. I'm free next Wednesday at 1:00 p.m.

Figure A4.6   Correspondence Log

L=Lead R=Referral	Name/Company	Telephone	Address	Result
L	John Smith RJ Company	342-5265	422 E. Drake Milwaukee, Wis	Set up 9/20 Lunch Meeting
R	George Astor Dan River Co.	462-4190	200 W. George Buffalo, NY	Meeting - Phone 10/21
R	Sharon Lang Smith Brenner	640-5710	2005 Tower Rd. Rolling Hills, IL	Call 2 Months 12/15

Resources and References

Buzan, Tony, *Use Both Sides of Your Brain.* 3rd ed. New York: Plume / NAL—Dutton, 1991.

Covey, Stephen R., *The Seven Habits of Highly Effective People.* New York: S & S Trade, 1989.

Csikszentmihalyi, Mihaly. *Flow, The Psychology of Optimal Experience.* New York: Harper, 1991

DeBono, Edward, *Serious Creativity, Using the power of Lateral Thinking to Create New Ideas.* New York: Harper Business, 1992.

Giovagnoli, Melissa, *101 Ways to MegaNetwork!* (tips booklet) Chicago: Practice Development Institute: (800) 227-0498.

Giovagnoli, M., and J. M.Moss, *The Chicago Entrepreneurs Sourcebook, Your Complete Guide to Starting Smart, Finding Resources for Growth and Creating Your Survival Network.* Chicago: Enterprise Dearborn, 1992.

Hyatt, C., and L. Gottlieb, *When Smart People Fail.* New York: Simon and Schuster, 1987.

Jeffers, Susan, Ph.D., *Feel the Fear & Do It Anyway.* New York: Fawcett Columbine, 1988.

Leanord, George, *Mastery.* New York: Plume, 1992.

Le Boeuf, Michael, Ph.D., *How To Win Customers & Keep Them for Life.* New York: Berkley Books, 1989.

Roane, Susan, *How To Work a Room, Learn the Strategies of Savvy Socializing for Business and Personal Success.* New York: Warner Books, 1989.

Roane, Susan, *The Secrets of Savvy Networking.* New York: Warner Books, 1993.

Schrage, Michael, *Shared Minds: The New Technologies of Collaboration.* New York: Random House, 1990.

Schwartz, David J., *Magic of Thinking Big.* New York: S & S Trade, 1986.

Slutsky, J., and Slutsky, M. *How To Get Clients.* New York: Warner Books, 1992.

Spina, Vicki, *Getting Hired in the '90s.* Corporate Image Publishing, 1992.

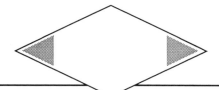

Index